THE
WICKED WIT OF
IRELAND

Also available
The Wicked Wit of England
The Wicked Wit of Scotland

THE
WICKED WIT OF
IRELAND

MYLES BYRNE

MICHAEL O'MARA BOOKS LIMITED

First published in Great Britain in 2019 by
Michael O'Mara Books Limited
9 Lion Yard
Tremadoc Road
London SW4 7NQ

A CIP catalogue record for this book is available from the British
Library.

Papers used by Michael O'Mara Books Limited are natural, recyclable
products made from wood grown in sustainable forests. The
manufacturing processes conform to the environmental regulations of
the country of origin.

ISBN: 978-1-78929-023-3 in hardback print format
ISBN: 978-1-78929-033-2 in ebook format

1 2 3 4 5 6 7 8 9 10

Designed and typeset by Design 23
Illustrations by Andrew Pinder

Printed and bound by CPI Group (UK) Ltd, Croydon, CR0 4YY

www.mombooks.com

CONTENTS

INTRODUCTION

The *Irish Independent* recently posed the question, 'What does it mean to be Irish?' inviting young people to post videos of their replies. The answers varied widely – some mentioned the vibrant and evolving culture, others harking back to traditional music and dance. There were a few mentions of the Irish mammy and the ever-present offer of a cup of tea or a drop of drink, a suggestion that Irish people tend to be 'chancers or risk-takers', with others saying you are 'probably Catholic but never go to Mass'. This matches the Irish writer Fiona Looney's recollection that 'As a teenager, I really only went to Mass to see ridey [attractive] young fellas.'

One of the overriding suggestions was that the Irish are defined by what they find funny, and expats have spread their wit and sense of humour right around the world. The vlogger James Mitchell said that 'as a nation, we have this fantastic, collective sense of humour'. He tells the story of an American talking to his holidaying father and telling him that she had just seen 'your Prince Harry' on television, to which his father responded by bursting out laughing. 'We are able to look at things from a different angle . . . we laugh at whatever we can just to make a situation better.'

In the same vein, the playwright Sean O'Casey once said: 'That's the Irish people all over – they treat a serious thing as a joke and a joke as a serious thing.' O'Casey carried this attitude into his own life, refusing to take anything too seriously and refusing to doff his cap to any man. In fact, he was fired from Eason's newspaper in the 1890s for refusing to doff his cap when he collected his wages. O'Casey's stubbornness stood out even at his wedding to the Irish actress Eileen Reynolds in the 1920s because he decided to wear 'a sweater'; he always refused to wear a dinner jacket, saying it was fit only for the coffin.

It is hard to pin down why humour is such a defining characteristic of Irish culture. And whatever reason one Irish person suggests, it will be easy to find another who disagrees. The Irish have the reputation of being especially disputatious – as George Bernard Shaw wrote: 'Put an Irishman on the spit and you can always get another Irishman to turn him.'

Shaw also had plenty of experience of the Irish tendency for taking the piss. At one meeting in London at which his fellow ex-pat Oscar Wilde was present, he suggested a new magazine. Asked what the title would be, he replied: 'Oh, as for that, what I'd want to do would be to impress my own personality on the public – I'd call it *Shaw's Magazine*: Shaw-Shaw-Shaw!' He banged his fist on the table to emphasize this. 'Yes,' replied Wilde, 'and how would you spell it?' It's reported that Shaw joined in with the laughter at him.

So, let's start by acknowledging that countries that are islands seem to have especially strong identities, possibly because they had isolated histories, resorting to ingenious means to survive. Ireland's history is a complex and often tragic one – there have been power struggles and battles at least since the Battle of Clontarf in 1014, and the British have been interfering in the country since the twelfth century, often with bloody results. The comedian Tommy Tiernan aptly commented: 'The English like to invade countries, but they get upset if they're followed home.'

In the nineteenth century, the potato famine led to a huge Irish diaspora, and a large expat population right around the world that continues to celebrate its Irish roots. And those roots were shaped by a long battle for independence, which has led to an island divided between two jurisdictions: the Republic of Ireland and Northern Ireland. They were also shaped by religious divisions, the political struggle between progressives and conservatives, and an often chaotic history.

Perhaps that complex history has led to the Irish mindset of finding humour in the darkest places, and refusing to take life too seriously or be ground down by misfortune. Brendan Behan, the great Irish writer, once wrote: 'When anyone asks me about the Irish character, I say look at the trees. Maimed, stark and misshapen, but ferociously tenacious.' Conor Cruise O'Brien wrote: 'Irishness is not primarily a question of birth or blood or language; it is the condition of being involved in the Irish situation, and usually of being mauled by it.' And Edna O'Brien regarded Irishness as being rooted in the whole experience of the Irish people: 'Other people have a nationality. The Irish and the Jews have a psychosis.'

But out of this national fascination with the morbid and unfortunate comes a great sense of absurdity and scepticism. The scholar John Dominic Crossan says that 'It's not that the Irish are cynical. It's rather that they have a wonderful lack of respect for everything and everybody.' One of Ireland's most successful recent exports, the musician Andrew Hozier-Byrne (aka 'Hozier') summed it up nicely in the song 'Take Me To Church', describing a lover who has a sense of humour as they 'giggle at a funeral'. And Hugh Leonard has pointed out how the Irish refuse to make a fuss about things: 'An Irishman will always soften bad news, so that a major coronary is no more than a "bad turn" and a near-hurricane that leaves thousands homeless is "good drying weather".'

That sense of the absurd also lends itself to a wonderful ability to marry together the sacred and the mundane. The comedy *Father Ted* rests on this contrast, between the pomposity and self-importance of a certain type of Catholic priest and the sheer ludicrousness of moments like Ted's attempt to teach Dougal about perspective by showing him a toy cow: 'These cows are small. But those are *FAR AWAY*!'

In James Joyce's *Ulysses*, the humour is often as

black as the sea at Dun Laoghaire on a November night: when Leopold Bloom and Stephen Dedalus are casually discussing the time when a coffin fell from its carriage in a Dublin street, they ask whether the solution is a 'funeral tram track'. And at Paddy Dignam's funeral, Bloom finds himself pondering the horror of being buried alive and musing on whether telephones in coffins would be 'a good way to prevent this'. Joyce was always quick to find humour in any situation, and when a young man once approached him in Zurich and asked, 'May I kiss the hand that wrote Ulysses?' Joyce replied: 'No, it did lots of other things too.'

Many other classic Irish writers have used black humour, wit and sarcasm across the centuries, ranging from the satires of Jonathan Swift, George Bernard Shaw and Oscar Wilde, to the absurdism of Samuel Beckett and James Joyce, to the hilarity of J. P. Donleavy and the sublime nonsense of Flann O'Brien (pseudonym of Brian O'Nolan) and Spike Milligan – 'How long was I in the Army? Five foot eleven.' Frequently inspired by political and religious shenanigans, Irish literature and art have shown a joyous iconoclasm, as suggested by the Marian Keyes' quote: 'What doesn't kill us makes us funnier.'

This book combines a pinch of traditional Irish humour, mixed with modern one-liners, quips and quotes from the best of the current crop of humorists including Dermot Morgan, Pat Shortt, Sean Hughes, Brendan Behan, Chris O'Dowd, Denis Leary, Conan O'Brien, Cathy Kelly and many, many more. It includes sections on the Irish mammy, literary feuds and putdowns, anecdotes and epitaphs, and the great eccentrics of history.

We will be taking an overview of many different aspects of Irish culture and heritage from classic writers onwards. First, though, let's look at the great Irish art of taking the piss, then we'll return briefly to that complex history and saunter through a millennia of bloodshed, strife and black humour.

CHAPTER ONE

A FEAST
FOR WOLVES

Insults, Curses and Putdowns

---

*'Dublin University contains the cream
of Ireland – rich and thick.'*

SAMUEL BECKETT

Insults, putdowns and generally taking the piss are an integral part of Irish banter. Samuel Johnson once said: 'The Irish are a fair people, they never speak well of one another.' It has also been said that 'the Irish do not want anyone to wish them well; they want everyone to wish their enemies ill.' And the Argentinian writer Maria Brandan Araoz has written: 'If there were only three Irishmen in the world you'd find two of them in a corner talking about the other.'

THE FINE ART
OF TAKING THE PISS

It is seen as the right and proper thing to let people know directly or indirectly what you think of them. As the comedy singing group The Nualas once put it: 'There is no disagreement that can't be solved with a good cup of tea, in the face.'

Brendan Behan, that wasted talent of Irish literature, chose to do himself down in order to pre-empt others doing the same, saying: 'I am married to Beatrice Salkeld, a painter. We have no children, except me.' But at the same time he was willing to write off all of his countrymen in a single throwaway line: 'If it was raining soup, the Irish would go out with forks.' Meanwhile, Flann O'Brien was happy to address the readers of his newspaper column (under the pseudonym Myles na Gopaleen) in familiarly insulting terms: 'You smug, self-righteous swine, self-opinionated sod-minded suet-brained ham-faced mealy-mouthed streptococcus-ridden gang of natural gobdaws.'

James Joyce was similarly unkind when he declared that 'Ireland is the old sow that eats her farrow'. And the novelist Joseph O'Connor has laid into modern-day Dublin, saying it resembles 'Disneyland with super-pubs, a purgatory open till five in the morning'.

Indeed, many of the most subtle Irish insults can be mined from its literary scene. Consider the subtlety of another Flann O'Brien quote, again implying his superiority over his audience: 'I saw that my witticism was unperceived and quietly replaced it in the treasury of my mind.' O'Brien could be equally cutting in person: for years he combined the writing life with working in the civil service, and when his habit of insulting senior politicians in his column finally provoked his bosses into firing him, one of his colleagues recalled him departing 'in a final fanfare of f***s'.

'While they may be descended from the Celts, a fearless people whose warriors were known to run naked into battle, most modern-day Irish people would think twice before running naked into the bathroom.'

FRANK McNALLY

THE YOUNG YEATS

Seamus Heaney was a serious poet, but he liked to tell funny anecdotes as much as the next man. He once recounted the story of a senior Irish literary figure who was at a dinner party, along with the young W. B. Yeats. Yeats then cut an affected figure in his fancy cape, had a lock of hair carefully trained to fall over his brow and always had a distant, arty air about him. Next day, the senior writer was asked: 'Well, you've met the young Yeats – what did you think of him?' Heaney would start laughing as he gave the reply in a hyped-up Irish accent: 'Think of him? *Think* of him, is it? I think he should be put back in and fooked-for again!'

HATERS GONNA HATE

The literary scene has always been bitchy, going back to some of the greats of Irish literature including those, like Oscar Wilde, who decamped to other countries. Wilde famously said that 'America is the only country that went from barbarism to decadence without civilization in between.' It was also Wilde who described another expat, George Bernard Shaw, thus: 'Bernard Shaw is an excellent man; he has not an enemy in the world, and none of his friends like him.'

Shaw warned against the danger of getting into slanging matches: 'Never wrestle with pigs. You both get dirty and the pig likes it.' However, he was himself the author of numerous stinging ripostes. Of rich people he said: 'To be clever enough to get a great deal of money, one must be stupid enough to want it.' He attacked economists: 'If all economists were laid end to end, they would not reach a conclusion.' And he was especially scathing about nationalists, suggesting that 'Patriotism is your conviction that this country is superior to all other countries because you were born in it,' and going further to declare that 'patriotism is a pernicious, psychopathic form of idiocy'. In spite of having moved to England, he also said: 'The English have no respect for their language, and will not teach their children to speak it.' (Kenneth Tynan summed up the importance of figures such as Wilde and Shaw when he said: 'It is Ireland's sacred duty to send over, every few years, a playwright to save the English theatre from inarticulate glumness.')

*'The Irish gave the bagpipes to the Scots as a joke,
but the Scots haven't seen the joke yet.'*

TRADITIONAL JOKE

DEAD AS DOORNAILS

Anthony Cronin's memoir *Dead as Doornails* is a wonderful account of some idiotic and drunken times spent in the company of Brendan Behan, Flann O'Brien and the poet Patrick Kavanagh. One day in McDaid's (their regular Dublin haunt), a young *gurrier* (i.e. a hooligan or tyke) tells the barman that Kavanagh has gone to the zoo 'looking for drink'. The response is: 'I wonder they didn't keep him there. I suppose they thought he might frighten the animals.' Later in the same passage, Kavanagh accuses a fellow Dubliner of being a bore. 'Oh, come on now, Paddy,' said one of the group. 'You can't say that, everyone knows he's a brilliant talker. After all, he successfully talks for his dinner.' Kavanagh's response: 'He'd eat a damn sight more if he kept his mouth shut.'

'True friends stab you in the front.'

OSCAR WILDE

A TRACE OF SLIME

Samuel Beckett is thought of as a highbrow, serious kind of writer, but he actually has a typical Irish ability to use black humour in his writing. For instance, his 1946 short story, *The End*, contains the memorable lines: 'The earth makes a sound as of sighs and the last drops fall from the emptied cloudless sky. A small boy, stretching out his hands and looking up at the blue sky, asked his mother how such a thing was possible. "F*ck off," she said.'

Beckett could also be quite self-deprecating. When once complaining about writer's block to the director Peter Brook, Beckett noted: 'I feel like a snail, but, as such, you have to leave a little trace of your slime behind you.'

EIGHT GAELIC CURSES

Go mbrise an diabhal do chnámha
May the devil break your bones

Mallacht mo chait ort
My cat's curse is upon you

Droch chrích ort
A bad ending upon you

Loscadh is dó ort
May you be burned and scorched

Go mbrise an diabhal do dhá chois
May the devil break your legs

Go dtuitfeadh an tigh ort
May your house fall upon you

Nár chuire Dia ar do leas thú
God will never grant you peace

Go ndéana an diabhal dréimire do chnámh do dhroma
May the devil make a ladder out of your spine

THE CRITIC'S BURDEN

Unsurprisingly, for a nation where a common saying is that a critic is 'a person who will slit the throat of a skylark to see what makes it sing', there is little love lost between Ireland's writers and critics. Brendan Behan described critics as being 'like eunuchs in a harem: they know how it's done, they've seen it done every day, but they're unable to do it themselves.' Yeats had a wider swathe of the fourth estate in his sights when he said: 'A journalist invents his lies, and rams them down your throat.'

Of course, no one likes a bad review. As the author and critic Rosita Sweetman says: 'Most of us hate criticism. If a friend approaches proclaiming: your hair looks crap. Your arse is getting awful big. And that colour does NOT suit you, would you break into the *Hallelujah* chorus? I don't think so.' Moreover, the Irish writing scene is a notoriously small place where you are likely to run into enemies. Éilís Ní Dhuibhne is one writer who is at least prepared to admit how personally she takes a bad review: 'I hate the reviewer forever and plot acts of revenge. Usually I plan to accidentally throw a glass of red wine over them at a book launch. Or else trip them up as they browse in Books Upstairs – on the stairs.'

'Journalism, the only job that requires no specialized knowledge of any kind.'

PATRICK CAMPBELL

HOWLING WOLVES

Of course, it's not just the writing community that can suffer from a bad review. When Hotel Doolin in the West of Ireland received a bad review on TripAdvisor, the general manager, Donal, felt obliged to respond directly, disputing the facts.

Having suggested that the review revealed a lot of suppressed anger, he revealed his own method of dealing with rage: 'Sometimes at night . . . I go out into the field at the back of my house and scream into the darkness. I let it all out, like a wolf on a moonlit mountain. I feel better after that and nobody gets hurt. I'm not saying howling into the night like a wolf will work for you . . . but there are other ways of channelling rage that don't have to involve Hotel Doolin . . .' He went on to express confusion at the reviewer's reference to several grumpy old men working at the hotel as there were only three employees over the age of forty, but then said that his assistant manager had found a solution.

'We've decided to execute all three of these men to ensure that no other guests will have to endure the horrific ordeal you went through that evening in the bar.' He promised that all three would be blindfolded, then shot in the back of the head after Mass the following Sunday, with the event being accompanied by trad music, cocktail sausages and face-painting for the kids. He even offered the former visitor a pair of complimentary tickets, while regretting that this harsh punishment wouldn't be sufficient to make up for the customer's bad experience – but hoping it might at least be a start.

'"That was excellently observed", say I, when I read a passage in an author, where his opinion agrees with mine. When we differ, there I pronounce him to be mistaken.'

JONATHAN SWIFT

CUSSING AND DISSING

Insults and ancient curses, such as 'you shit of a crane' and 'may your body be a feast for wolves', have a long heritage in Irish history. In the Celtic sagas, Ferdia, the warrior of Connacht, taunted Cúchulainn, his Ulster opponent, calling him a 'chicken-hearted coward'. Other early curses included 'May the raven of the battlefield be joyful over your breast' and 'Slow speech on your descendants forever'. In the medieval period it often fell to bards to include poetic insults in their songs, and one is reputedly the origin of the proverbial curse: 'May the cat eat you and the devil eat the cat.'

'May the curse of Mary Malone and her nine blind illegitimate children chase you so far over the hills of Damnation that the Lord himself can't find you.'

BARDIC CURSE

HALLIONS AND SLABBERS

Flann O'Brien had a scathing opinion of the politicians of his time, saying: 'The majority of the members of the Irish parliament are professional politicians, in the sense that otherwise they would not be given jobs minding mice at crossroads.'

Modern politics remains a farcical affair, and is also fertile ground for insulting speeches and statements. Remember Bertie Ahern telling Gay Mitchell, 'You're a waffler, you've always been a waffler, you've been hanging around here for years, waffling', and Michael McDowell adding insult to insult by calling Mitchell the 'evil of two lessers'. Even better, Ian Paisley once characterized Cardinal Cahal Daly as 'the red-hatted weasel of Armagh'.

Charles Haughey was another well-known politician who had a poisonous way with words. He claimed only to have gone to the funeral of his contemporary Erskine Childers 'to make sure the f**ker was dead' and described another politician as 'the nastiest piece of work to crawl in here'. And Mary O'Rourke, referring to Ruairi Quinn, once said: 'Deputy Quinn persistently seeks to act out his political life as a misplaced character from *Noddy Gets Narky*, and I for one have had enough.'

It's also worth recalling the words of Una Bean Mhic Mhathúna, the campaigner for family values, who reacted to the aftermath of the 1995 divorce referendum by calling the people campaigning for divorce 'wife-swapping sodomites'.

> *'The reason there are so few female politicians is that it takes too much time to put make-up on two faces.'*
>
> MAUREEN MURPHY

ALL THE WORLD'S A STAGE

The world of theatre also provides fruitful ground for insults. For instance, Colin Farrell is one actor who receives much opprobrium for being 'more Irish in Hollywood than he ever was at home in Dublin'. Farrell likes to recount the first time he met Donald Sutherland, with whom he was making a film. Sutherland's first five words to him were: 'Put that f**king cigarette out.'

Richard Harris once wrote off the entire world of actors, saying 'they'd go to the opening of an envelope. Any big occasion, they're always there. Anything for exposure. We can do without them. Actors are unimportant.' When Harris was working with Charlton Heston in the 1959 seafaring epic *The Wreck of the Mary Deare*, he took a strong dislike to the famous actor, saying: 'He'd played in Shakespeare and to listen to him you'd think he helped the Bard with the rewrites.'

Harris engaged in trench warfare directed at Heston, summing up their relationship thus: 'He was a pr*ck, really, and I liked tackling pr*cks.'

INSULTS: AN IRISH LEXICON

The Irish have a wide array of everyday insults for every occasion: 'You're as thick as manure but only half as useful'; 'He's so cheap he'd live in your ear'; 'He wouldn't give the steam of his piss to the clouds if he thought it'd make rain'; 'As slow as a wet week'; and 'She could peel an orange in her pocket'. So here is a handy guide to some more common Irish insults.

Gobshite: a mortal insult for someone who talks nonsense (as in, 'He's an awful feckin' gobshite')

Gobdaw (from the Gaelic gabhdán): a gullible person

Scut: a useless, lazy person

Gombeen: a chancer or shady person

Septic: adjective for an affected or insincere person

Ghoul (or 'ghoul-bag', for emphasis): an idiot

Gowl: a clumsy person

Gurrier: a hooligan

Eejit: a fool (used, for instance, by Father Ted's Father Jack when he is being attacked by birds – 'Feckin' feathered eejits! Gobshites, the lot of ya!'

Pup: immature brat

Lickarse: sycophant

Maggot: an irritating person

Langer: offensive Cork term for a fool

Dry shite: boring, humourless person, so one of the worst possible things you can accuse an Irish person of being

'It was hard not to admire her intelligence, her iron will, her confidence and control. But all in all I thought she was a bit of a wanker.'

DAVE FANNING,
AFTER INTERVIEWING MADONNA

THE BURNING CAKE

Con Houlihan was a much-loved Irish sports journalist whose best writing soared to the heights of poetry. Writing, for instance, about the Kerry vs Dublin All-Ireland football final 1978, he wrote: 'Mike Sheehy was running up to take the kick – and suddenly Paddy [Cullen] dashed back towards his goal like a woman who smells a cake burning. The ball won the race and it curled inside the near post as Paddy crashed into the outside of the net and lay against it like a fireman who had returned to find his station ablaze.'

So remarkable was his ability to convey the atmosphere of a sporting occasion, one participant in an online forum said: 'I am reminded of the story when a man returning from a game was once asked what he thought of the match. "Sure, how would I know until I read what Con has to say about it?" was the reply.'

'*I came to Ireland about six weeks after you beat Romania in the World Cup – and about eight weeks before you stopped celebrating.*'

DES BISHOP

THE SAIPAN INCIDENT

For now, let's give the final word to a master of the scabrous rant, the footballer Roy Keane. He was captain of the national team, then preparing on the island of Saipan for the 2002 World Cup, but was so unimpressed by the team's preparations he gave an interview to the *Irish Times*, making his reservations known. When manager Mick McCarthy called him out during a team meeting, this was Roy's memorable response, which led to his departure from the team and return home without having kicked a ball. 'Mick, you're a liar . . . you're a f**king wanker. I didn't rate you as a player, I don't rate you as a manager, and I don't rate you as a person. You're a f**king wanker and you can stick your World Cup up your arse. The only reason I have any dealings with you is that somehow you are the manager of my country! You can stick it up your b*llocks.'

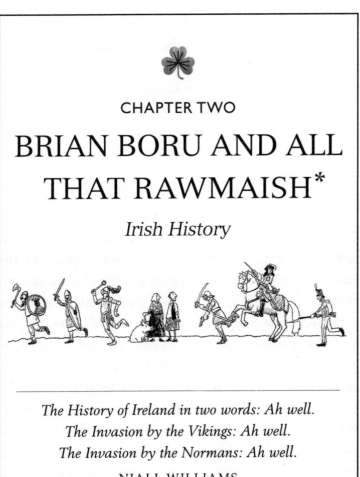

CHAPTER TWO

BRIAN BORU AND ALL THAT RAWMAISH*

Irish History

The History of Ireland in two words: Ah well.
The Invasion by the Vikings: Ah well.
The Invasion by the Normans: Ah well.

NIALL WILLIAMS

---

*Rawmaish (noun): Irish foolish or exaggerated talk; nonsense

29

Niall Williams' parody of the stereotypical Irish response to their history continues by listing other notable events such as 'the Flight of the Earls', 'Mr Oliver Cromwell', 'the Famine', 'the Troubles', 'the Church', 'the Banks' and 'the eight hundred years of rain' before again concluding: 'Ah well.' But there is also much to be proud of in Irish history. Here's a quick skim through the millennia.

THE EMERALD ISLE

Who the earliest settlers were is unknown, but they date back about 10,000 years to a period when the weather was so cold that the seas around the British Isles and Ireland were frozen. It was possible for travellers to walk across both the English Channel and the Irish Sea, but if they were in search of better weather they would have been sorely disappointed. As Mary Mannion said: 'The only thing you can say for sure about the Irish weather is there's nothing you can say for sure about the Irish weather.'

The Christian Church had become the dominant religion by the seventh century AD, replacing earlier forms of Celtic paganism. It launched a period of great confusion in Irish history. Saint Patrick, the patron saint of Ireland, is reputed to have cleared the island of snakes in the fifth century and to have been the founder of the Christian religion there. However, he may well not have existed at all and, if he did, he could have been either Scottish or Welsh. An old poem, attributed to William Maginn, runs:

You've heard of St Denis of France,
He never had much for to brag on.
You've heard of St George and his lance,
Who killed old heathenish dragon.
The Saints of the Welshmen and Scot
Are a couple of pitiful pipers,
And might just as well go to pot
When compared to the patron of vipers:
St Patrick of Ireland, my dear.

THE PEACEFUL YEARS

The early Christian Church in Ireland wasn't stupid and incorporated many elements of the old Celtic culture into its rites, including (allegedly) transforming the spring goddess Brigid into St Brigid. Legend or not, she seems to have had a sense of humour. She wanted to build a monastery, so kept asking King Leinster for some land. After several refusals, she cunningly asked him for a piece of land 'as big as my cloak'. Thinking that she was either joking or mad, the King finally assented to her demand, at which point she laid out her cloak and it turned out to cover acres of land. Jesus can keep his fishes and loaves, Brigid's giant cloak is far more impressive.

The monasteries of Ireland were then great centres of learning (and Ireland

Bugger

was significantly more civilized than the British Isles, where the Dark Ages were in full swing), which attracted students from across Europe. Part of the history of early Ireland was recorded in the florid prose of the Irish sagas: the brilliant writer Flann O'Brien was fond of parodying them by putting preposterous speeches into the mouth of the mythical hunter-warrior Finn MacCool.

In one passage in *At Swim-Two-Birds*, MacCool is asked to describe the sweetest music he has ever heard. Part of his reply is: 'I like gull-cries and the twittering together of fine cranes. I like the surf-roar at Tralee, the songs of the three sons of Meadhra and the whistle of Mac Lughaidh . . . I incline to like pig-grunting in Magh Eithne, the bellowing of the stag of Ceara, the whinging of fauns in Derrynish. The low warble of water-owls in Loch Barra also, sweeter than life that.' The list continues with examples such as 'wing-beating in dark belfries', 'the whining of small otters in nettlebeds at evening' and 'the chirping of little red-breasted men in bare winter'.

One reason why these centuries were so peaceful was that the Romans never crossed the Irish Sea to invade. This is partly down to a historic example of fake news. The Romans had been convinced, possibly by a cunning Irishman in a Londinium bar, that Ireland was a nation of cannibals. Fearing for their lives, they decided to leave Ireland, along with Scotland, in the 'crazy dangerous Celtic' drawer.

Beautiful times, indeed.

*'Isn't it a very curious thing that St Patrick
drove the snakes out of Ireland an' the
English brought in the fleas.'*

FRANK McCOURT

THE BIRTH OF THE BRAWL

The peaceful centuries, when Finn MacCool's beautiful
sounds were supposedly commonplace, were brought to an
end with the arrival of the Vikings. Irish schoolchildren
tend to learn a simplified version of this period, including
the story in which Brian Boru liberated his countrymen
with a great victory at the Battle of Clontarf. Inevitably the
truth is more slippery – Boru was also in conflict with the
powerful Uí Néill dynasty, and Danes fought on both sides
in the skirmishes that ended the power of those descendants
of the (possibly mythical) 'Niall of the Nine Hostages'.

As Con Houlihan wrote in the *Irish Herald*: 'We saw
this as a kind of European Cup final between Ireland and
Denmark and were delighted that we had won. Brian, we
were told, was slain while praying in his tent after the battle
but this was probably another example of spin doctoring.'
Houlihan continues with the murkier truth, arguing that
the Danes weren't defeated and continued to be important
traders, and that 'centuries went by and battles succeeded
battles and wars succeeded wars and in all those years the

island of Ireland was never a single political entity.'

A traditional Irish joke relates how an American tourist buys the 'genuine' skull of Brian Boru in an antiques shop for just a few hundred euros. Returning the next year, he is offered a slightly smaller 'genuine' skull of Brian Boru in the exact same shop. When he protests that he is being cheated, the shopkeeper placates him saying: 'Ah, but this one is the skull of Brian Boru when he was a boy.'

'Never hit an Irishman when he's down.
He might get up again.'

SEAMUS O'LEARY

MEDIEVAL MONKS

The famous, decorated manuscript, the *Book of Kells*, contains some surprising moments of sly humour that seem to have been slipped in by the monks to amuse themselves while working on the more serious parts. The book includes a lot of ornamental Celtic knotwork, but you also find weird little figures with their legs folded into knots and tongues tied into bows. There is also one tiny figure drinking a goblet of wine, eyes closed (apparently in a drunken stupor) and failing to notice the huge monster with gleaming teeth that is creeping up behind him. And some of the finest moments in the monk's humorous asides concern increasingly surreal details, such as warrior

rabbits, giant snails and figures holding trumpets to their buttocks in what appears to be an early example of the fart joke.

THE BLARNEY STONE

According to legend, if you kiss the Blarney Stone (an old stone in the battlements of the eponymous castle), you gain the gift of the gab. But don't go near. You might as well go to Disneyland, so clogged up with tourists has the place become. It's just an old stone, anyway, and why would you want to kiss it? Someone recently asked the contributors to an internet forum if it was true that the locals tended to piss on the stone for laughs. One deadpan response was: 'Not intentionally. But sometimes, when you're taking a shit, it just happens.'

THE ENGLISH ARRIVE

The Norman invasion from Britain in the late twelfth century was the start of many centuries in which the British interfered with Ireland and its culture, often to dreadful effect. Part of the early motivation was for the English Church to gain control of that of Ireland: one history notes that the English demanded 'the abandonment of features of Gaelic society going back to pre-Christian times and of practises which had been accepted for centuries by the church in Ireland.' It says a great deal about Irish resilience that this was never fully achieved. The situation naturally became more complex after the Church of England separated from the Catholic Church under Henry VIII, with many subsequent problems revolving around attempts to suppress the stubborn persistence of Catholicism in Ireland. (The humorous book *1066 and All That* sums up Henry VIII's approach to Ireland by saying that he was 'very good at answering the Irish question, and made a law called Poyning's Law, by which the Irish could have a parliament of their own, but the English were to pass all the Acts in it. This was obviously a Very Good Thing.')

James Joyce memorably summed up the attitude of many Irish people to the British: 'The British beatitudes are beer, beef, business, bibles, bulldogs, battleships, buggery and bishops.' During one particular period of turmoil in England, the Irish attempted to take their chances with the Irish Rebellion of 1641. As long as the English were busy fighting each other this coup held, but Oliver Cromwell then brutally suppressed the revolt, gave large amounts of land in the North to his Protestant supporters and created the conditions for even worse problems to come.

One traditional joke describes Cromwell's army sweeping across Ireland, before halting outside Cork. Cromwell asks: 'What is the problem?' The answer: 'It's Big Mick, the Prince of Cork, he's in this cave and we can't get him out!' At this point Big Mick is heard bellowing and demanding Oliver's toughest man be sent in. So a huge soldier enters, armed to the teeth, but is heard being overcome.

Big Mick then shouts for Cromwell to send in his five next toughest men, then his next twenty, easily defeating them each time. However, one Roundhead survives the last spat and scrambles out, bleeding from head to toe. He crawls his way to Cromwell and says: 'Sire, don't send in any more men. It's a trap – there's two of them!'

'The Englishman has all the qualities of a poker except its occasional warmth.'

DANIEL O'CONNELL

THE RARE OULD TIMES

In 1782 Ireland finally had a functioning parliament, with control over its own army. It was known as Grattan's Parliament after Henry Grattan, a reforming campaigner and leader of the Patriot Party. Among its many provisions, the new constitution gave the Parliament greater control over the Royal Irish Army. On the same day, Mulligan's pub opened in Poolbeg Street in Dublin.

Sir Boyle Roche, MP for Tralee in Kerry, is remembered for his cack-handed speechmaking in subsequent years. He once told his audience that 'the cup of Ireland's misery has been overflowing for centuries and is not yet half full.' If that mixed metaphor wasn't enough, he went on to claim that 'all along the untrodden paths of the future, I can see the footprints of an unseen hand.'

Unfortunately, the culture of drinking outlasted that outbreak of home rule. Mulligan's pub is still open today, but the Parliament only lasted a few years, being abolished following the 1798 uprising by the United Irishmen.

'This may come as a surprise to generations of Irish pupils, but the Irish language wasn't invented just to infuriate people forced to learn it at school.'

DARACH Ó SÉAGHDHA

A CATHOLIC ATHEIST OR A PROTESTANT ATHEIST?

The nineteenth century saw the ongoing suppression of Irish culture, with the language and traditions being kept alive only by the hedge priests, who taught in the countryside, traditionally underneath or behind hedges, although they often stayed out of the rain and found refuge in huts or shelters. It also saw the potato famine, during which boatloads of the crop continued to be sent to England while tens of thousands of Irish people starved or left the country to try to find a better life abroad. In *1066 and All That*, the authors continue the story, saying that the British Prime Minister Gladstone 'spent his declining years trying to guess the answer to the Irish Question; unfortunately, whenever he was getting warm, the Irish secretly changed the Question.'

After a long political campaign, the fight for Irish independence erupted in 1916 with the Easter Rising that led to a kind of independence (which gradually solidified) for the Republic of Ireland, but also resulted in partition from the North. It also cemented the divide between nationalist and unionist, Catholic and Protestant, and so led to the Troubles in the latter part of the century. There is little funny that can be said about that.

The broadcaster and writer Rachael English has written: 'I still hold two truths with equal and fundamental certainty. One: the British did terrible things to the Irish. Two: the Irish, had they the power, would have done equally terrible things to the British.' She does, though, go on to give the British a backhanded compliment: 'It is impossible not to admire a people who gave up India and held on to Northern Ireland. That shows a truly Celtic sense of humour.'

The Catholic/Protestant rift has also given rise to the following, related by Richard Dawkins. A journalist trying to get a story about the complex political situation is visiting a pub in a dangerous, sectarian area of Belfast. His potential informant is suspicious of him and wants to establish his credentials.

'Are you a Catholic or a Protestant?'

'Neither,' replied the journalist, 'I'm an atheist.'

The Irishman still isn't happy and asks a further question: 'Ah, but are you a Catholic atheist or a Protestant atheist?'

'The main difference between wives and terrorists is that you can negotiate with terrorists.'

FRANK CARSON

THE BIGOT ON THE BRIDGE

A popular internet joke takes the question of sectarianism even further. A man sees another man on a bridge, about to kill himself, and begs him not to:

'Why shouldn't I?'

'Well, there's so much to live for!'

'Like what?'

'Are you religious?'

'Yes.'

'Me too. Are you Christian or Buddhist?'

'Christian.'

'Me too. Are you Catholic or Protestant?'

'Protestant.'

'Me too. Are you Episcopalian or Baptist?'

'Baptist.'

'Wow. Me too. Are you Baptist Church of God or Baptist Church of the Lord?'

'Baptist Church of God.'

'Me too. Are you original Baptist Church of God, or are you Reformed Baptist Church of God?'

'Reformed Baptist Church of God.'

'Me too. Are you Reformed Baptist Church of God, Reformation of 1879, or 'Reformed Baptist Church of God, Reformation of 1915?'

'Reformed Baptist Church of God, Reformation of 1915.'

To which the first man says 'Die, heretic scum!' and pushes the other off.

PEACE IN OUR TIME

I was recently reduced to tears by an Irish musician, who grew up during the Troubles in Belfast, explaining how his twelve-year-old daughter had just asked whether there used to be some kind of war there. The beautiful thing is that she had grown up with so little consciousness of it that this was the first time she had even mentioned it. Thankfully, the 1998 Good Friday Agreement brought peace and has held.

And while British politicians in the Brexit era seem determined to re-enact the kind of Keystone Cops chaos that Irish politicians have perfected over the decades, hopefully the progress that has been made in Ireland will continue. The Irish language has survived and is prospering, the Troubles are over, we have seen some action on the scandals of abuse in the Catholic Church, the ban on abortion has been overturned in the South, gay marriage has been legalized and we have lived through one of the most prosperous periods in Irish history (notwithstanding the minor blip of the property crash and global financial crisis). But comedy is never far away: recently the Irish government accidentally made drugs legal for twenty-four hours.

'They're selling crack in my neighbourhood. Finally.'

KEVIN BRENNAN

ME, FEISTY?

Of course, the Irish will always be capable of finding a new dispute. As Austin O'Malley wrote: 'An Irishman can be worried by the consciousness that there is nothing to worry about.' Yes, Ireland has come to feel like a much more modern, progressive country, one that is at home in Europe and finally free of some of the shackles of history. Or, as Frank McNally put it, the 'land of saints and scholars has become a land of limousines and lap dancers'. Disputes? Con Houlihan once wrote about meeting an immigrant from the Philippines who told him: 'I am no longer a Philippina. I am a little Irish girl.' He added: 'There is only one fault I can find with these people: they speak English so well that sometimes I find it hard to understand them.'

CHAPTER THREE

CEOL AGUS CRAIC
The Craic and Paddywhackery

'God then made man. The Italians for their beauty.
The French for their cuisine. The Welsh for their
voices. The Germans for their cars. And on and
on until He looked at what He had created
and said, "This is all very well, but no one
is having fun. I'll have to make an Irishman."'

TRADITIONAL JOKE

Let's get this out of the way. For purists of the Gaelic language, the word 'craic' (which is pronounced 'crack', and roughly translates as 'good times and banter had by all') is not what most people think it is. Professor Diarmaid Ó Muirithe described the word as 'a hideous neologism'. It has also been called 'fake Irish', 'pseudo-Gaelic' and 'a linguistic lie'. This all seems a bit harsh for such a harmless, positive word, but there is some truth in it. The word was rarely used in Ireland before the late 1960s, yet the word 'crack' has been used in Scotland and northern England for centuries to mean much the same thing. Walter Scott used it in *Rob Roy*, the Scottish poet Ebenezer Picken mentioned 'the friendly crack' and Robert Burns defined it as 'to chat, to talk'.

The word seems to have travelled to southern Ireland via Ulster. An anthology of humour entitled *Brave Crack!* came out in 1951, and the word was in general use across the island by the 1960s and 1970s. The Gaelicized version of the word dates back to the late 1960s when an advertisement in Irish referred to the *ceol agus craic* (or fun) in Irish pubs, and the marketing of Irish pubs around the world in the 1990s relied heavily on this phrase. It was also used as part of a catchphrase in a chat show on RTÉ television. Of course, there are limits to the craic, with one Irish proverb proclaiming that 'every man is sociable until a cow invades his garden'.

*'If anyone complains that they're feeling a bit drunk
too early at your party, just show them Shane
McGowan and say, "That's what pissed is.
How do you feel now?" They'll say, "Much better
thanks. I'll have a triple vodka."'*

PAT FITZPATRICK

'THE CRAIC WAS NINETY'

Possession is nine-tenths of the law, and its current use in Ireland is a reflection of a culture that genuinely values good company and happy times, with one traditional proverb suggesting that 'Continual cheerfulness is a sign of wisdom'. When people meet up they might ask: 'How's the craic?' (meaning 'How are things?'), 'What's the craic?' ('What's happening?') or 'Any craic?' ('Is there any gossip?').

A great time, possibly but not necessarily in the pub, can be referred to as 'great craic'. Or you can describe such fun by saying 'the craic was mighty' or even 'the craic was ninety' (a reference to the 1960s Barney Rush song, 'The Crack was Ninety in the Isle of Man', which used the English spelling).

Irish people have taken the word to heart and many don't even know its non-Irish origins, precisely because it is such a good reflection of their way of life. And that way of life involves the recent revival of traditional music and the possibility that an evening in the pub might turn into a spontaneous ceilidh. As Roddy Doyle once wrote: 'To claim that music is more important than oxygen would be trite and sentimental. It would also be true.' And the oldest fiddles are indeed often the sweetest: some of the traditional Irish songs have been sung at gatherings for centuries.

'A man from Manchester once told me he once approached a barman in a small village in the West of Ireland at one o'clock in the morning and asked what time the pubs closed. "October", he was informed.'

PETE McCARTHY

'WE ALL PARTIED'

Even when things go wrong the idea of partying and having fun comes into the equation. Following the property crash of 2008–9, Finance Minister Brian Lenihan went on RTÉ's *Prime Time* to explain his recovery plan. He started out humbly enough: 'I accept that there were failures in the political system. I accept that I have to take responsibility as a member of the governing party during that period for what happened.' But then he blew it with the casual follow-up: 'But let's be fair about it. We all partied.' It was a bold but doomed attempt to appeal to the collective Irish sense of craic (it failed largely because not everyone had been invited to that particular party).

When James Reilly was health minister from 2011–14, he took this attitude even further. He was only trying to suggest that it was healthier to drink in social situations than at home, but was embarrassed when a newspaper headline read: 'Health Minister urges drinkers to return to the pub.'

'A good laugh and a long sleep are the two best cures.'

TRADITIONAL PROVERB

OIRISHNESS GALORE

Nothing irritates a Dublin taxi driver more than their fourth American tourist of the day claiming to be of Irish descent and demanding that he tell them where the craic is. In his *What it Means to be Irish* video, James Mitchell wonders why everyone seems to want to be Irish. 'I once had someone tell me they were Irish . . . [because] they loved the colour green . . . Seriously.' Even Barack Obama has got in on the act, introducing himself to the Irish public thus: 'My name is Barack Obama, of the Moneygall Obamas, and I've come home to find the apostrophe we lost somewhere along the way.' It is commonly said that 'there are only two kinds of people in the world: the Irish and those who wish they were'.

'With a hand full of beer and a heart full of cheer,
I'm as Irish as I can get, but add good times
and some quick funny lines ... and gold I make
leprechauns sh!t.'

JON BENDERA

FAR AND AWAY

It doesn't help that Irishness has been depicted in such a cutesified and bizarre fashion, especially by Hollywood. *The Quiet Man* (1952), with John Wayne, in which the genuinely Irish Barry Fitzgerald gives the stereotypical caricature performance of the Oirish priest, is a notorious example. Like many other films of the last fifty years it depicts all the Oirish as lovable rural rapscallions with green eyes who are always up for a drink, a song or a fight. That's because, as Dylan Moran points out, 'that's *still* how Irish people are seen, as twinkly-eyed f*ckers with a pig under their arm, high-stepping it around the world, going, "I'll paint your house now, but watch out, I might steal the ladder later, ohohoho!" Which is only half true!'

Some of the standard tropes of the Oirish film include a priest who turns out to be a handy fighter, the wicked English villain, beaten wives (often treated 'comically'), cute little girls who believe in leprechauns, angels and pots of gold at the end of the rainbow and sentimentality by the barrel. Of

the later examples, Philip Kerr has described *Far and Away* (1992), starring Tom Cruise and Nicole Kidman, as 'a filum so bogusly Oirish that it made *Darby O'Gill and the Little People* (1959) look like a documentary, begorrah.' The poor dialect coach Tim Monich had worked for seventeen years before taking on his first film involving Irish accents. Nicole Kidman's character is a well-to-do landowner's daughter, who would almost certainly have had a largely English accent, but she had to be given an Oirish version of a Dublin accent to avoid confusing international audiences.

The film is something of a cult classic in Dublin cinemas, where audiences gather to mock the accents. The mockery extends to Tom Cruise, and recent Irish Twitter threads were full of people explaining how Cruise had ruined their day. Eamon Gilmore complained that he had been told Tom Cruise was taller than him, @Paul-at-9 complained that he was still waiting for Cruise to buy his round after the last time while @RonanDusty expressed the deepest fear of many: 'Tom Cruise is in Ireland. Hopefully a *Far and Away* sequel will not be mentioned'.

'Hollywood is full of what we in Dublin call gobshites.'

PAT O'CONNOR

'TOP O' THE MORNIN' TO YAH'

Beyond Hollywood, Oirishness rears its head any time the tourist industry depicts Ireland as a land of shillelaghs, shamrocks, Blarney stones and Guinness. And it is displayed most egregiously in some of the St Patrick's Day parades around the world. The first of these actually took place in New York in the eighteenth century, not in Ireland where they are less stereotypical, even sober, affairs. The American versions tend to involve people, several generations removed from the actual island, dressed in green with leprechaun hats and fake shamrocks shouting clichés such as 'top o' the mornin' to yah' in Oirish accents that even Hollywood would reject.

One elderly Irish gentleman was recently stopped by a TV3 reporter and asked if he would be going to the St Patrick's Day parade. He replied: 'I'll be staying in my garden with my dog . . . if you ask me, it's the greatest load of ponce . . . all the Americans are over here sayin' "Aw my

Gawd, I lurve Oireland." It does my f**kin' head in.' So there you go.

If you do visit Ireland, it's best to avoid attempting the accent. If you've ever watched local news in America on St Patrick's Day or heard an Englishman attempting an Irish accent, you'll know how excruciating it can be to see people saying 'Begorrah!' and thinking they sound authentic. Don't talk about pots of gold at the end of the rainbow either. And, whatever you do, don't dress up in one of those dreadful leprechaun outfits that are found on the worst St Patrick's Day marches. It's best to avoid *'erin go bragh'* (i.e. Ireland until eternity; it's common in the US, but an anglicization). Basically, if you're thinking about trying any kind of Irish accent whatsoever, give yourself a long, hard look in the mirror and keep the gob shut.

'I never felt Irish. I always felt, "I'm English, this is where I come from, and that's that." Because you'd be reminded of that when you went to Ireland: "Ye're not Oirish!" the locals would say. So it was like, "Bloody hell, shot by both sides here".'

JOHN LYDON

DID YOU HEAR THE ONE ABOUT THE IRISHMAN ...?

Of course, the Irish did once contain some of the elements in these jokes. As long ago as the eighteenth century, the Scottish writer James Boswell claimed that 'the Irish ignore anything they can't drink or punch'. And the persistence of such tropes is also partly down to Irish comedians of earlier generations playing up Irish stereotypes. Hal Roach became hugely successful as a comedian in the 1950s and 1960s with an act that relied heavily on paddywhackery, telling stories when the Irishman was often the butt of the joke. He was especially popular with American tourists and coach parties in Ireland. And some of his jokes were actually making fun of Irish tropes, for instance: 'You know it's summer in Ireland when the rain gets warmer.'

A more typical Roach joke tells how Father O'Seamus asked the congregation at Mass to stand up if they wanted to go to hell. When Muldoon stands up, the priest asks if he wants to go to hell and he replies: 'No, Father, but I didn't like to see you standing there by yourself.' He also referred to a typical priest's housekeeper as 'sitting at the fire with two crowbars knitting barbed wire'.

'There is a man sitting in the middle of the road casting his fishing line . . . now none of us is perfect, but c'mon! So, I asked him, "How many have you caught today?" He said, "You're the ninth."'

HAL ROACH

'YOU JUST F**KING WATCH ME'

Of course, the stereotypical depictions of priests and housekeepers feed directly into the world of *Father Ted*. Dermot Morgan was keen to point out the distinction, explaining: 'It's not about "paddywhackery" clichés. It's essentially a cartoon. It's demented. It has its own world and as much integrity as *The Simpsons*.' The link between the two was emphasized by the appearance of Brendan Grace, a traditional comedian who started his career, strongly influenced by Roach, in the brilliant sitcom. Incidentally, Grace tells a joke about Irish astronauts building a rocket to fly to the moon using turf as fuel; when it is pointed out that the sun is extremely hot, they boast that's why they are going at night.

After Dermot Morgan died far too young, at the age of fifty, his son Don wrote: 'I can only assume he died, and that it wasn't a very sick joke on his part, although I wouldn't put it past him. He was a brat that way.' He also described his father's brutal education in which the Christian Brothers often beat him for his transgressions. One teacher shouted at him: 'Morgan, you'll never make anything of yourself.'

Dermot was 'presumably bypassing whatever part of your brain deals with self-preservation' when he answered: 'You just f**king watch me.'

PAT AND MICK

A glance through traditional Irish joke books, whether published in America, Britain or Ireland, will glean huge amounts of paddywhackery. Whether it be this joke, 'Overheard in O'Banion's Beer Emporium: "Pardon me, darlin', but I'm writin' a telephone book. C'n I have yer number?"' or those that rely on potatoes, something that 'Paddy' or 'Pat and Mick' said, or others featuring an Englishman, Scotsman and Irishman walking into a bar, they all feel increasingly remote from modern Irishness, which has left behind these stereotypes.

*'There's an intense cultural relevance being Irish.
You battle to keep that. Even at the risk of
being very obnoxious.'*

SHARON HORGAN

WHERE WE ARE NOW

Happily, the current generation of comedians and writers is increasingly confident of being able to represent Ireland in its true, modern form. Comedians and writers as varied as Dylan Moran, Sharon Horgan, Tommy Tiernan, Alison Spittle, Graham Linehan, Arthur Mathews, Chris O'Dowd and Ed Byrne have their own distinctive ways of celebrating and mocking their origins, while still occasionally acknowledging the rain-soaked, Guinness-sodden Oirish paddywhackery of old.

CHAPTER FOUR

A PINT OF PLAIN

Drinking in Ireland

'*Moderation, we find, is an extremely
difficult thing to get in this country.*'

FLANN O'BRIEN

An integral part of craic is, of course, the drinking. And drinking is an art that has been taken to great heights in the Emerald Isle as well as by the Irish abroad. As Spike Milligan once said: 'Many people die of thirst but the Irish are born with one.'

THE VIEW FROM THE PERCH

My wife once discovered a tiny, probably unlicensed, bar run by an elderly Irish lady hidden in a basement off the North Circular Road in London. There was a magnificent green macaw loose at the end of the bar. After eyeing up my wife and her friends, it sidled along the counter to approach them and then started to talk in an impeccable Irish accent. 'Get out, you're feckin' drunk', then 'You feckin' drunken bastards!' As it continued with the expletives, the landlady fondly told them that he had lived in the bar for ten years and had picked up quite a few phrases.

The centrality of drinking in Irish culture is reflected in the many proverbs that mention it, such as: 'May the enemies of Ireland never eat bread nor drink whiskey, but be afflicted with itching without the benefit of scratching.' (Whiskey is spelt with an 'e' because Irish whiskey is 'extra special'.) And I recently saw a tea towel in a giftshop full of Oirish artefacts that read: 'Drink is the curse of the land. It makes you fight with your neighbour. It makes you shoot at your landlord. It makes you miss him.'

Along with drinking comes the singing. Just think

of how many classic Irish songs are about drinking or prominently feature alcohol: 'Beer, Beer, Beer', 'The Irish Rover', 'Whiskey in the Jar', 'All For Me Grog', 'Seven Drunken Nights' . . . the list is long enough to sustain an all-night drinking session. And the greatest Christmas song of all time, 'Fairytale of New York' by the London-Irish Pogues, starts out in the drunk tank in New York and goes on to picture all the drunks singing, and Sinatra swinging. Shane MacGowan, who wrote the song, is notorious for his excesses – he apparently once ate a Beach Boys record while drunk.

In one interview, while discussing the fact that Shane was still going strong twenty-five years after being given six months to live, the interviewer asked if there was any rock star – such as Iggy Pop or Lou Reed – who could outdrink him. When he insisted there wasn't, his girlfriend Victoria humorously suggested that Kate Moss could not only 'wipe the floor' with him but drink loads and still be photographed looking fantastic for the cover of *Vogue* in the morning. Shane replied: 'I've been on the cover of magazines looking fantastic, having drunk f**king enormous amounts. No one's ever beaten me in a proper drinking competition.'

'Everyone drinks . . . Well, unless they don't.'
SHANE MacGOWAN

WRITERS' RUIN

Drinking and literary culture have often gone hand in hand, and a standard saying is: 'If an Irishman says he's a writer, give him a sobriety test. If he flunks it he's telling the truth.' Of course, it's a fine line between drunkenness and alcoholism. Brendan Behan was a brilliant writer, capable of writing the extraordinary *The Quare Fellow* (his first play). However, his life became a performance of drunken antics and mayhem, far beyond the usual craic and good times, especially after a sodden 1956 appearance on Malcolm Muggeridge's BBC *Panorama* programme.

Muggeridge later wrote: 'One drunken, speechless television appearance brought more of the things he wanted, like money and notoriety and a neon glory about his head, than any number of hours with a pen in his hand.' He was similarly intoxicated when he appeared on Edward R. Morrow's show *Small World* in 1959. The American comedian Jackie Gleason, who had also been on the show, said: 'Behan came over one hundred per cent proof. It wasn't an act of God, but an act of Guinness.'

BLUEBOTTLE SQUADRONS

Flann O'Brien was another literary great who, arguably, squandered part of his talent due to a fondness for the whiskey. James Joyce described O'Brien's masterpiece *At Swim-Two-Birds* as having the true comic spirit. And his newspaper columns (under the byline Myles na Gopaleen) were enduringly hilarious, with his bizarre flights of fancy, ludicrous puns and constant bickering with 'the Plain People of Ireland'. He once wrote: 'No genuine Irishman could relax in comfort and feel at home in a pub unless he was sitting in deep gloom on a hard seat with a very sad expression on his face, listening to the drone of bluebottle squadrons carrying out a raid on the yellow cheese sandwich.' But some critics argue that writing the columns and spending the rest of the day drinking was the main reason why he never finished more than a handful of books.

SPANNERED, STEAMIN' OR BALOOBAS?

Bill Barich's excellent book on the Irish pub takes its name, *A Pint of Plain*, from Flann O'Brien's poem, 'The Workman's Friend'. He discusses the wide range of words for drunkenness in the Irish language: 'They're spannered, rat-arsed, cabbaged, and hammered; ruined, legless, scorched, and blottoed; or simply trolleyed or sloshed. In

Kerry, you're said to be flamin'; in Waterford, you're in the horrors; and in Cavan, you've gone baloobas, a tough one to wrap your tongue around if you ARE baloobas. In Donegal, you're steamin', while the afflicted in Limerick are out of their tree.'

'Here's to a long life and a merry one. A quick death and an easy one. A pretty girl and an honest one. A cold pint and another one!'

IRISH PROVERB

THIS SPORTING LIFE

Drinking has even played a prominent part in sport in Ireland. One of Northern Ireland's most famous exports was the magnificent George Best, who was notorious for his drinking, even in his playing days. After his retirement he famously said: 'I spent a lot of money on booze, birds and fast cars. The rest I just squandered.'

Snooker player Alex Higgins was another flawed sporting great, who is remembered mainly for his drinking and carousing. It was ironically said of him that 'Alex Higgins isn't looking too well recently. He's obviously not getting enough greens.' Higgins once drank twenty-seven vodkas during a single snooker match. Unsurprisingly, it was the drinking and smoking that ended his career and probably killed him at just sixty-one.

His fellow snooker player John Virgo remembers visiting Higgins after the latter had won the World Championship. Far from the luxury that might have been expected for a world champion, Virgo found himself in a 'crummy flat' with congratulatory telegraphs littering the floor, and the trophy left casually on a sideboard. Spotting a small saucer of cheese among the detritus on the floor, Virgo asked what it was for. Higgins explained he didn't want the flat's resident mice population to starve.

DON'T ASK, DON'T TELL

When it comes to acting, Richard Harris always had a nice line in self-deprecation: 'I formed a new group called Alcoholics Unanimous. If you don't feel like a drink, you ring another member and he comes over to persuade you.'

Peter O'Toole explained the way that the post-show comedown drove some to drink: 'There are some who kick the dressing-room door to splinters. Some go home and savage a spouse. Others quit the stage doors with all convenient speed, find themselves holes wherein they may safely skulk, there get pissed as rats.'

Michael Caine tells a story from his early acting life, when he was the understudy to O'Toole in *The Long and the Short and the Tall* at the Royal Court theatre, in 1959. O'Toole invited Caine out to dinner and offered him a plate of chips. Caine could remember nothing after except waking up in a flat he didn't recognize two days later, at

5pm, with only three hours left to recover and get back to curtain-up. 'Never ask what you did,' O'Toole said. 'It's better not to know.'

Father Jack: *'Drrrriiink!'*
Father Ted (panicking): *'Don't drink that, Father! No, it's . . .'*
Father Jack: *'FECKIN' WATER!'*

FROM *FATHER TED*

HAIR OF THE DOG

Ireland is famous for its stout, and it is often said that 'an Irishman is the only man in the world who will step over the bodies of a dozen naked women to get to a bottle of stout.' When Peter O'Toole was once asked his favourite Irish food he answered: 'My number one choice is Guinness. My number two choice would be Guinness. My number three choice would have to be Guinness.' (Note: Guinness is not the only stout – residents of Cork swear by Murphy's, which is their city's version.) Many jokes take a similar theme, for instance the old quip that 'only Irish coffee provides in a single glass all four essential food groups: alcohol, caffeine, sugar and fat.'

Whiskey is also a favourite tipple. Mark Twain once wrote: 'Give an Irishman lager for a month, and he's a dead man. An Irishman is lined with copper, and the

beer corrodes it. But whiskey polishes the copper and is the saving of him.' Furthermore, it is often said that 'Irish whiskey was first developed for its medicinal benefits. It's just lucky for the rest of us that the Irish are such a sickly bunch.'

In the end, the main thing with drinking, in spite of Flann O'Brien's lament about the lack of moderation in Ireland, is that in sensible quantities it can contribute greatly to the craic. J. P. Donleavy, author of *The Ginger Man*, famously wanted to go on helping his compatriots after he departed, writing that 'when I die I want to decompose in a barrel of porter and have it served in all the pubs in Ireland.' It isn't recorded whether his wish was granted, but there are still plenty of pubs in which a glass was raised to him after he left this mortal coil.

Sláinte! ('Cheers' in Gaelic)

'"Drink never drowns anyone's sorrows," he went on. "It only teaches them how to swim."'

MARIAN KEYES

CHAPTER FIVE

I TOLD YOU
I WAS ILL

Death, Funerals and Epitaphs

*'What's the difference between an Irish wedding
and an Irish wake? One less drunk.'*

TRADITIONAL JOKE

If we must die (and I have it on good authority that we must), then one of the best ways to depart this world for the afterlife is via an Irish funeral. The Irish long ago perfected the art of combining mourning with celebration and giving the deceased a good send-off. Perhaps this is because, as a Catholic and somewhat morbid nation, the Irish have an everyday acquaintance with death and greet its arrival with weary resignation rather than as a bolt from the blue.

*'I watched a funeral go by and asked who was dead.
A man said: "The fella in the box."'*

TRADITIONAL JOKE

THE FUNERAL LINE

A friend of mine was once visiting a great aunt in hospital in Dublin, when her older cousin Philomena, whom she hadn't met for years, arrived. Philomena is the traditional Irish mammy, in her early sixties and an incorrigible gossip. On this occasion, she set off entertaining the great aunt with tales of people they used to know. 'You know Peggy O'Mara, the one who was friends with Sally in the village store?' The great aunt, who was not in great shape, would nod in recognition before Philomena continued. 'Dead. Pneumonia over that terrible winter last year. And you know Iris, the one who lived up at the big house on the hill until her husband died and she took up with that widower?' The great aunt nodded. 'She's dead. She had a heart attack.' The litany of deaths continued, and seemed to give both parties much satisfaction, until finally Philomena mentioned someone of my friend's age whom she had played with as a child. 'You know Rose, the one who went off to Dublin and then moved back to the end of the road?' My friend said: 'I remember her. How is she?' The answer: 'Dead, in a car crash. It was an awful shame …'

This fascination with who has died and who might be next, plays a part in the funeral ritual. Kevin Toolis, author of *My Father's Wake*, notes that local radio stations in Ireland still have deaths announcements. For instance, Midwest Radio (the Mayo country and western station) has one three times a day, listing the deaths and funeral arrangements of those who have recently departed. (Rural Ireland is, of course, sparsely enough populated for this to be feasible.) Toolis adds: 'There is even a phone line, ninety-five cents a minute, just so you can check up on those corpses you might have missed.'

'Curran said to Father O'Leary, the wittiest priest of his day, "I wish you were St Peter." "Why?" asked O'Leary. "Because," said Curran, "you would have the keys of heaven, and could let me in." "It would be better for you," said O'Leary, "that I had the keys of the other place, for then I could let you out.'

W. R. LeFANU

BEING THERE

Once the funeral announcement has been made, you have to decide who is going to the wake, who is going to the Mass and who is driving who to what. This is a complex task requiring many phone calls and texts, as it is extremely important not just to go and pay your respects but to be seen doing so.

Comedian Pat Shortt, who has toured a comedy show in which he performs as the singing undertaker Mossey Burke, tells the story of a shopkeeper from Thurles who had a special funeral coat always at the ready in his shop, from which the church was visible. Any time a hearse arrived, he closed up, put the coat on and hurried across the road, 'hand outstretched, to offer his condolences. You'd often see the coffin tilt and sway as the men carrying it reached out to shake hands. Now that's how you get to be seen at a funeral!'

'My grandmother made dying her life's work.'

HUGH LEONARD

SORRY FOR YER TROUBLES

A traditional Irish wake is held in the home, with an open coffin. This means that people will be keenly aware of how expensive your coffin is. The Irish poet, Sigerson Clifford, left extensive instructions regarding this issue, saying he didn't want a costly coffin: 'If a plain box is good enough for the Pope, a middle price coffin is good enough for me. Too good, maybe. Soon as the coffin arrives pop me in, screw down the lid and tell those who want to stare at me to shove off. When they didn't come to admire me when I was worth looking at, I don't want them peering at me when I can't see what they're thinking about me.'

Nonetheless, the wellwishers and mourners will turn out, and a surreal experience it will be. Where else in the world do you arrive at the house, get handed a cup of tea and a ham sandwich, mumble 'sorry for your loss' or 'sorry for yer troubles' and then pay your last respects with children playing around the foot of the coffin table? Bear in mind that this may well be the moment you realize that the priest has tightly wound that lovely antique rosary that Aunty Becky promised you around her hands. You will probably only consider untangling it very, very briefly: and at least this way you won't have to bicker with the cousins over who she really promised it to. Also bear in mind that it is traditional to note what a lovely job the undertaker has done.

The comedian Dave Allen once attempted to explain the Irish wake to his English audience: 'In Ireland when somebody dies, we lay 'em out and watch 'em for a couple of days,' he said, going on to explain that, 'if anybody else anywhere in the world dies, that's the end of it, they're dead.' However, in Ireland: 'It's a party. It's a send-off. The fella is laid out on the table and there's drinking and dancing and all the food you can eat.'

It is also standard etiquette to comment favourably on

the suit or dress that the deceased is wearing. At a friend's grandfather's wake a major row was triggered by the simple phrase that it was 'a shame for someone to be buried in such a good suit'. This inevitably led to accusations that it was an insinuation that the suit had actually been promised to the speaker, and that they were being cheated by the use of it in the coffin. Fortunately, time heals all wounds and by midnight the warring parties were doing the 'rowing the boat' dance on the floor together.

'The thing about Anna is that she can be acutely
perceptive, but she's not great on practical things.
Like remembering to get dressed before
leaving the house.'

MARIAN KEYES

THE WRONG WAKE

Pat Shortt also tells the story of his aunt's wake: she was a popular woman so there was a good turnout. One woman that he didn't know barged her way to the coffin, gave his auntie a kiss and set off chatting to all and sundry. Eventually she had another look in the coffin and with tears in her eyes said: 'God bless him but didn't he get very grey in the end? I'd hardly recognize the poor man.' She'd actually come to the wrong wake.

The coffin tends to be removed in the evening, ready for the funeral the next day, giving those who have to work a last chance to turn up late and then, quite possibly, head for the pub to discuss what a lovely person the deceased was. This alternates with uproarious recollections of that time they did something incredibly foolish on holiday, or that car they bought that fell apart the very next day. And the doctors also get a mention. These notes are taken from patients' medical records:

While in the ER, she was examined, X-rated and sent home.

By the time he was admitted, his rapid heart had stopped, and he was feeling better.

Discharge status: Alive but without permission.

'There's one thing about a late marriage –
it doesn't last long.'

ELDERLY IRISHMAN ON RTÉ

A GIGGLE AT A FUNERAL

The funeral itself will often teeter dangerously close to the edge of hysteria. Any inadvertent double entendre from the vicar during his encomium of the deceased, any stumble from the bereaved family or inappropriate shout from a child ('Mummy! I want a drink!') will set shoulders heaving in the back row and beyond. At one funeral I went to, the weird spectacle of the priest chucking holy water at the coffin set off a major commotion as a second cousin of the deceased commented: 'You'd think the coffin was on fire the way he's chucking that water at it.'

PRANKS

There is an increasing tendency for the family, sometimes acting on the explicit instructions of the dying relative, to play things up with practical jokes. Undertakers report an increase in the use of inappropriate songs at the most solemn moments, such as 'Ring of Fire' by Johnny Cash, Rod Stewart's 'Maggie May' ('Wake up, Maggie . . .') and

Wham!'s 'Wake Me Up Before You Go-Go!' The mobile phone of the deceased has even been placed behind the coffin and dialled at an opportune moment.

Hal Roach once defined the funeral tribute as 'one man lying in a coffin and another lying on the altar'. But, in general, the speeches are not the reverent affairs we find in some countries – it's more likely that the anecdotes from the pub the night before will get another outing, along with the story about that time the eejit tried to drive down the road to the shop and ended up backing the car into the duckpond.

Afterwards, while the Irish mammies are still congratulating the vicar on his lovely words, comes the race to the pub and the bitter grumbling at anyone who has beaten you to the pile of ham and cheese sandwiches. This would be the appropriate moment to start asking . . . Who all the friends and relatives actually are? Who is related to who? Who has died since the last funeral? Who might be next?

And finally comes the drinking and dancing. Time to let your hair down, bring out the truly inappropriate anecdotes about the individual who is leaving this mortal coil and to give them a real send-off.

'I was at a wake the other night and every man jack was drunk – even the corpse.'

FLANN O'BRIEN

FUNNY EPITAPHS
(from *Dead Funny* by Allen Foster)

Erected to the memory of JOHN PHILLIPS, accidentally shot as a mark of affection by his brother.

Here lies John Highey, whose mother and father were drowned in their passage from America. Had they both lived they would be buried here.

Here lies the body of Thomas Kemp, lived by wool died by hemp [At the grave of a man hanged for sheep stealing.]

Beneath this stone lies Katherine my wife
In death my comfort, and my plague through life
Oh liberty! but soft I must not boast
She'll haunt me else, by jingo, with her ghost

Here lies the remains of John Hall, grocer. The world is not worth a fig. I have good raisins for saying so.

Here lies poor but honest Cecil Pratt. He was a most expert angler until death, envious of his merit threw out his line and hooked him.

This stone was raised to Sarah Ford, not Sarah's virtues to record – for they're well known to all the town. No Lord; it was raised to keep her down.

LAST, LAST, LAST RITES

Of course, the fascination with funerals can lead to some odd bits of behaviour. One of my relatives, Jessie Heneghan, used to be something of a hypochondriac. This was back in the days when the Catholic Church would only administer the last rites before death, so there was a great fear that if you died suddenly you might be delayed on your journey to heaven, or never get there. Every time Jessie had a cold she would retire to bed, phone her friends to declare that the end was approaching and demand the attendance of the priest, who would come and dutifully go through the motions. I remember the day after one of these dramatic interludes my nan telling my granddad that she had seen Jessie.

'How's she holding up?' he asked.

'She can't be too bad, I guess, I ran into her in the cake shop.'

'My granddad died in his rocking chair. I didn't know it would keel over when I climbed on the back.'

MICHAEL REDMOND

DÚIRT MÉ LEAT GO RAIBH MÉ BREOITE

And the last word should go to Spike Milligan, who is remembered among many other things for the epitaph he requested for his gravestone: 'I told you I was ill.' This was the headline on Britain's *Daily Mirror* on the day his death was announced. There was a bit of a tussle between the family and Chichester diocese over the use of the epitaph in the graveyard, before it was resolved – the English words 'Love, light, peace' give a suitably solemn feel to the stone, while the Gaelic version of 'I told you I was ill' (*Duirt mé leat go raibh mé breoite*) also appears.

It seems that humour is allowed in the graveyard, but only if it is wrapped up in the Irish language.

CHAPTER SIX

FATHER BLACKJACK
AND
FATHER WHITEWASH

The Church

---

*'I have nothing against the Church as long
as they leave the drink alone.'*

BRENDAN BEHAN

My wife's Irish grandfather used to grumble about the parish priests who would wander the streets looking for their prey, generally older members of the flock who might give them a cup of tea and listen to their piety for a while. 'Here they come,' he'd say, 'Father Blackjack and Father Whitewash.' Blackjack was the drinker, the smoker and the straight talker, while Whitewash spent many a Mass boring the congregation to tears with his platitudes and waffle.

Anyone with a Catholic childhood will recognize the odd assortment and types of priests that he was parodying, and which is captured so brilliantly in the television series *Father Ted*. It's actually hard to think of the Church in Ireland without being reminded of this great sitcom that skewers the small-town priest's mentality so deftly. (It's also hard to think of the Church without remembering the many scandals and outrages that have marred its recent history: there's not a great deal of humour to be found there, although Sean Hughes had a go with 'the Catholic Church has a new policy on child abusers: three strikes and you're a cardinal.') At one point, Ted explains Catholicism succinctly: 'That's the great thing about Catholicism, it's so vague and no one really knows what it's about.'

Dermot Morgan, who is best known to British audiences for his role as Ted, is also remembered fondly in Ireland for his many comic TV performances, including his character of Father Trendy, who would attempt to put Christian ideas into a radical, modern form in a doomed attempt to be down with the kids. One sermon included the line: 'We are all fishing for something in our lives, and what is it we are all fishing for?

That's right, *sole* . . .' And even more laboured is: 'Do you go to parties and go around like a Volkswagen? One clutch after another? Are you a JCB? A Jesus Christ Believer? Or does your religion need a BMW? A bit more work?'

Relics: People who have been going to Mass for so long, they actually know when to sit, kneel and stand.

(FROM THE *ALTERNATIVE CATHOLIC DICTIONARY*)

A DOUBLE DOSE OF ORIGINAL SIN

Dylan Moran explains religion nicely: 'Look at the Catholic Church, the campest organization on the planet with the purple robes, gold bits on the side, jewellery so big if they let it fall it would kill people . . . What else can it be, but this sort of ritual of panic about death? "DEATH IS COMING! Quick, put on the gold hat!"' He also likens evangelists who tell you to let God into your heart to people who think that if you pray really hard a fairy will come to your garden: '"You have to let the fairy into your heart". Look, I wouldn't let him into my garden, okay? I'd shoot him on sight, if he existed, which he doesn't.'

The Church has always loomed large in Irish life – its suppression when England ruled the island means that it was inextricably caught up in the struggle for independence and the national identity that emerged (especially as many

Protestants either left the country or moved to the North after 1921, fearing that their country no longer belonged to them). For a long time, most legislation, including that on abortion and divorce, was based on Catholic doctrine. And daily life in rural Ireland in particular still revolves around the Church.

One old joke pictures two Irishmen considering going into the priesthood, chatting and comparing the Jesuit and Dominican Orders. One points out that they were both founded by Spaniards – the Dominicans by St Dominic and the Jesuits by St Ignatius of Loyola. In addition, they were both formed to fight against heresy – the Dominicans to fight the Albigensians and the Jesuits to fight the Protestants.

'So what's the difference?' asks one. The other drily responds: 'Met any Albigensians lately?'

'I'm an atheist and I thank God for it.'
GEORGE BERNARD SHAW

THE HOOLIGAN BEHAN

Of course, not everyone loves the Church. My wife's grandfather, for example, was an atheist Maoist, who nonetheless was given a Catholic funeral by his Irish family, which was conducted by a bad-tempered priest who couldn't keep himself from mentioning her granddad's non-attendance at Mass. The grandfather would have approved of Brendan Behan, who rejected all forms of authority with drunken disdain and boasted that he had 'a total irreverence for anything connected with society, except that which makes the road safer, the beer stronger, the old men and women warmer in the winter, and happier in the summer.'

On arriving at the Spanish border in the Franco era, Behan was asked about the purpose of his visit. 'We're here for Franco's funeral,' he said. The shocked guard told him that the General was very much alive. 'It's OK,' he replied, 'we can wait.' He didn't make it into the country.

On another occasion, in Dublin, Behan accosted the carol singers on Grafton Street – they were holding placards with religious mottoes on them. Behan seized one and tore it up, shouting 'Chairman Mao Tse Tung will soon put a stop to your f**king gallop, ye creeping Jesus's ye.' He then sprinted in the direction of Stephen's Green with several carol singers pursuing him.

After hiding in a bush, Behan nearly made it to the Russell Hotel in the company of Anthony Cronin, who had managed to avoid being identified as the atheistic communist's companion. The carol singers spotted Behan on the way in and a few ineffectual punches were thrown.

He stumbled into the lobby and started bolting the doors behind him. 'Get the rozzers! I'm a Dubbelin man and I'll show these bogmen that there's law and order in this town.' When the police arrived, he informed them that he had been set on for no reason by several men whom he suspected of being members of 'a rural-based organization of fascistic tendencies'.

No arrests were made.

Dougal: *'God, Ted, I've heard about those cults.
Everyone dressing in black and saying our
Lord is coming back to judge us all.'*
Ted: *'No . . . no, Dougal, that's us. That's
Catholicism you're talking about.'*

FROM *FATHER TED*

SOME SAY THE DEVIL IS DEAD

God and the devil play a part in many traditional Irish sayings, for instance: 'May you be at the gates of heaven an hour before the devil knows you're dead!' Another is: 'May those that love us love us, and those that don't love us, may God turn their hearts. If He can't turn their hearts, may He turn their ankles, so we'll know them by their limping!' One graveyard epitaph dedicated to a surly security guard reads: 'What a pity Hell's gates are not kept by O'Flynn, the surly old dog would let nobody in.'

The devil is also a regular feature of Irish folktales and songs, including the somewhat misogynistic 'The Women Are Worse Than the Men'. It's the story of a woman who is sent to hell. After making a nuisance of herself with all the demons and imps, the devil sends her back to her husband saying: 'Now, I've been a divil the most of my life, But I ne'er was in Hell till I met with your wife.'

'Did you hear about the man who couldn't keep up the payments to his exorcist? He was repossessed.'

NOEL V. GINNITY

TWO NUNS

There's an old Irish-American story about two nuns in a convenience store on a hot day. They are talking about the heat and discussing whether it would be wrong to buy a few beers and drink them on a bench in the sunshine. The first nun is doubtful, fearing that there will be problems if they are spotted buying alcohol, but the second nun has a plan.

She marches up to the counter, where the clerk does indeed look surprised at the beer she has plonked down there.

'I didn't know you were allowed to drink,' he says.

'Oh, we don't drink it,' she says. 'We use it to wash our hair. We call it Catholic Shampoo.'

'I see,' he smiles. He adds a box of pretzels to the bag, takes her money and says: 'The Catholic curling tongs are on the house.'

BELLS AND SMELLS

In the end, the Irish attitude to religion can be summed up in a couple of traditional saws: 'God is good to the Irish, but no one else is; not even the Irish.' Maybe that's why they hang on to a religion that merges the miraculous and sublime with the mundane and absurd. Or maybe it simply suits their self-deprecating sense of humour to have a religion where men dress up in robes and gold hats and dispense blessings from God while bells are rung, altar cloths are slung and incense is swung. And, in the end, you don't have to take it all *too* seriously: as the saying goes, 'There's no reason to bring religion into it. I think we ought to have as great a regard for religion as we can, so as to keep it out of as many things as possible.'

CHAPTER SEVEN

ROCKING THE SYSTEM

Irish Women

*'I was elected by the women of Ireland,
who instead of rocking the cradle,
rocked the system.'*

MARY ROBINSON

The election of Mary Robinson as Ireland's first female president in 1990 sent a powerful message about the status of women in Ireland. She was only the seventh president in Ireland's history, so that is as though Andrew Jackson had been Annabel Jackson. Robinson resigned in 1997 and went on to work as UN High Commissioner for human's rights, where she continued fighting for the rights of workers and women.

There have been some dark times for women in the past – scandals such as the Magdalene Laundries show that women, especially the poor or unmarried, were often treated atrociously. But Ireland's women are anything but weak, and Rosie Hackett, who was prominent in the Easter Rising, barricaded Liberty Hall in 1917 and afterwards scathingly pointed out that it took 'four hundred policemen to take four women'. In more recent times, Irish women have fought their way through to win referenda on issues such as divorce and abortion, and to play an increasingly prominent role in Irish culture and politics.

'Even if a man could understand women,
he still wouldn't believe it.'

NIALL TOIBIN

CALL FOR REINFORCEMENTS

The author Iris Murdoch, who was born in Ireland, compared the status of women to Irishness in general: 'I think being a woman is like being Irish. Everyone says you're important and nice, but you take second place all the same.' So it's best not to cross an Irish woman. A traditional Irish joke makes the point more forcefully: a Garda recruit is sitting his exam and asked what he would do if he had to arrest his own mother: 'Call for reinforcements.' And, according to Mignon McLaughlin, 'the only mothers it is safe to forget on Mother's Day are the good ones'.

And while on the subject of aggression, Conan O'Brien's talk show in America once had an absurdly Oirish St Patrick's Day item, including a dancing leprechaun interrupted by a (supposedly) Irish 'member of the audience', who proceeded to lecture Conan on the difference between fake and real Irish. One of the examples given of real Irish was 'getting into a bar fight with a girl and, when she beats you, asking her to marry you'. And while it's not often that one turns to the girl group *B*witched* for feminist inspiration, their biggest hit 'C'est La Vie' does include the lovely line, 'I fight like my da as well'.

---

*'Women see things that men don't: dirt,
relatives, bargains.'*

DYLAN MORAN

THE STRONGER SEX

Even some of the jokes that edge towards misogyny reflect the combative nature of Ireland's women: an old toast proclaims, 'Here's to our wives and mothers: may they never meet' while, in Brendan O'Carroll's joke, 'I love to praise my wife. She's gorgeous. She's wonderful. She's listening.' And then there's the traditional Irish comic Noel V. Ginnity's crack: 'Murphy came home from work and got a terrible shock. His wife said she wasn't leaving him.' That's echoed by Joe Lynch's line: 'My wife and I were blissfully happy for twenty years. Then we met each other.'

Even the women of earlier generations found their own little ways to rebel and escape from normality. John B. Keane once wrote that 'I think the Irish woman was freed from slavery by bingo . . . They can go out now, dressed up, with their handbags and have a drink and play bingo. And they deserve it.'

Another step into the modern world, propelled by a referendum, is the fact that Ireland now allows gay marriage. Mary Kenny's wry comment reflects the history of joking about marriage in Ireland: 'I believe in gay marriage. Why shouldn't they have to suffer like the rest of us?' Leo Varadkar recently became the first Taoiseach to address the crowd at Gay Pride in Dublin, on a day when the wit of the Irish was on full display as the floats passed close to Christ Church cathedral with 'Papa Don't Preach' blaring out of their speakers at full volume.

'A study in the Washington Post *says that women have better verbal skills than men. I just want to say to the authors of that study: Duh.'*

CONAN O'BRIEN

THE IRISH MAMMY

Even the much-mocked (and loved) Irish mammy is a stereotype that arises from the central place of the mother in Irish families. The apron-wearing mother with often-permed hair, who is permanently boiling bacon and cabbage and fussing about everything and nothing has been parodied on TV in everything from *Mrs Brown's Boys* to *Fifty Ways to Kill Your Mammy*. In his *What it Means to be Irish* video, Niall Gleason introduces his own 'Mammy Gleason', who lists the four things she always offers visitors to their home: 'tea, a drop of drink, food and a big welcome'.

One of the funniest mams in fiction features in Marian Keyes' books about the Walsh family. Mammy Walsh is a pitch-perfect character, unknowingly hilarious and touching at the same time. A lot of the humour is in the rhythms of her speech:

My sister Kitty brought us Vermouth from the
time she went to Rome and met that married
man, but the less said about that the better.
Mr Walsh's secretary (you were allowed to say
'secretary' in them days, not like now when it's
personal assistant this, personal assistant that)
used to go to Hungary and brought back a bottle of
Hungarian slivovich . . . The thing is no one *drank*
any of this stuff, no one was *meant* to drink any
of this stuff. They were ornaments, fine glittery
ornaments, in the same way my Aynsley vase was
an ornament until Claire threw it against the wall
and smashed it, the time her husband left her for
their downstairs neighbour, Denise . . .

Incidentally, if you haven't read any Marian Keyes because
she is a 'chick-lit' writer, think again. She's one of the
funniest Irish writers around, also being searingly honest
about the likes of alcoholism, depression and domestic
violence. Keyes may describe herself as an 'eejit who was
buying shoes the day Life's Rulebook was issued', but it's
not all cupcakes, chocolate cravings and twee romance in
her fictional world. And she can be pretty acerbic, saying
for instance: 'A lot of young women today say they want
to be writers when what they really mean is they want to
be published. They want the fame but not the hard work.
They want to be on *The Late Late Show*. They give me a big
fat pain in the arse.'

THINGS IRISH MAMMIES SAY

A letter came in the post for you, will I open it?
(Which means she already has.)

Close the door! Were you born in a barn?

How was your 'party'? I suppose there was
drink taken.

Do you think I'm made of money?

Eat that all up! Think of the starving children
of Africa.

*Take off your coat or it'll be no use to you
when you go outside.*

What did your last maid die of?

Don't make a show of yourself.

There's enough dirt in those ears to grow potatoes!

If I've told you once, I've told you a thousand times.

What's for you won't pass you by.

Don't eat those biscuits. They're for the visitors!

Who's 'she'? The cat's mother?

When I was your age we played with sticks and stones.

How do you know you don't like it if you
haven't tasted it?

Oh, so you're off gallivanting again I suppose!

That was a very quick mass.

I don't care what the other children's mammies
are saying. I'm not them.

While you're under this roof . . .

*'I always, always want to make people laugh. In
every situation. Even when it's inappropriate.'*

SHARON HORGAN

THE MODERN WORLD

So, the modern Irish woman finds herself dealing with the whole absurd mix of traditional Irish values and the social media age. There's also the question of how to age gracefully and whether the transformation into an Irish mammy is inevitable. As Sharon Horgan said: 'You feel you can pretend to be young until you're fifty, but after that what happens and how do you approach it?'

Horgan is an example of the increasing role of women as comedians: 'I think that's important to women in comedy, that we get a lot of the good lines and you're not just the girlfriend or the sister.' But how you can do this and retain a strong Irish identity? 'I think the best comedy is tragicomic. Yeah, I suppose if you were to look at everything I've done, there is a bit of a black streak through all of it. It's not deliberate: it's what makes me laugh, and there's a fine tradition of it, especially in Ireland.'

Many of the funniest and bleakest moments in her shows are based loosely on incidents in real life. It's unclear whether the moment in *Catastrophe* when Rob Delaney proposes to her, then drops the engagement ring in a puddle of urine (prompting her response, 'I love it. It's only a bit of piss.') was so inspired, although she reports her husband went pale when he saw the first episode and recognized moments from their own marriage. She has, however, confirmed that an after-show party for the boy band Take That inspired the moment in *Pulling* when, after a long night drinking, Karen looks down and says: 'Whose f**king knickers are these?'

'Being a mother sometimes means doing things you don't like. While changing a nappy once, I ended up with poo in my mouth. Don't ask me how.'

FIONA LOONEY

IRISH WOMEN TWEETING

Every Irish woman who's ever looked twice at a fiddle is getting accused of ridin' #EdSheeran #GalwayGirl

JOANNE MCNALLY

Whenever I hear people say they're off to do coffee runs I think: 'Woah, too much information there! And if it doesn't suit you, don't drink it.'

AMY HUBERMAN

I'm eating a breakfast roll while wearing spanx.
It feels like a civil war down there.

ALISON SPITTLE

Did a rape joke tonight. Thought only 22yo
over-indulged boy comics did that. What am I?
The genderbending benjamin button
of irish comedy?

ELEANOR TIERNAN

In the same way I hear the sea when I hold a
shell up to my ear, I hear my name whispered
when I hold up an almond croissant.

AMY HUBERMAN

Listening to filthy Prince songs on the dart.
I keep fearing a flash orgy.

ALISON SPITTLE

CHAPTER EIGHT

THE IRISH ROVERS

The Diaspora

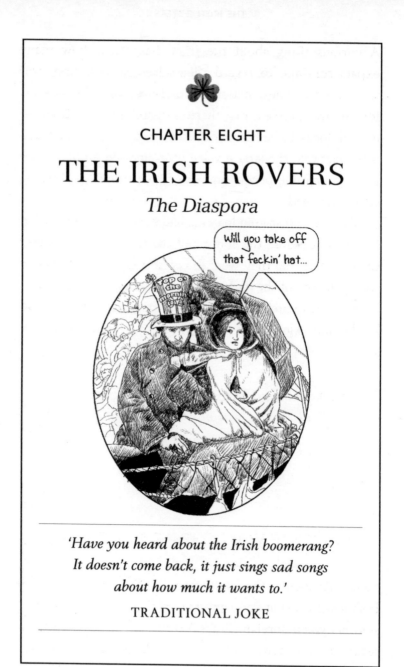

'*Have you heard about the Irish boomerang?
It doesn't come back, it just sings sad songs
about how much it wants to.*'

TRADITIONAL JOKE

A curious thing about the Irish diaspora is how many expats continue to regard themselves as Irish first, and whatever their new nationality is as second. The reasons for this are complex: first there is the old phrase, 'If you're enough lucky to be Irish, you're lucky enough!' Then there is the fact that the largest wave of emigration, in particular from the famine period onwards, was primarily driven by economic need.

My wife's great-grandparents had a successful horse farm in Wicklow before the coming of the motor car decimated their industry, so they were forced to move to Manchester where the site of the dark satanic mills along the canal must have made a depressing contrast with the green hills they had left behind. Along with many others, the family retained a strongly Irish culture for several generations in exile.

'I showed my appreciation of my native land in the usual Irish way by getting out of it as soon as I possibly could.'

GEORGE BERNARD SHAW

'A COAT YOU CAN'T TAKE OFF'

Laura Kennedy, the *Irish Times* columnist, describes Irishness as 'a coat you can't take off', and which starts to smother you in foreign climes. While awaiting her brother's return to the homeland after a spell abroad she wrote:

'I would like my brother's return to Ireland to have the poetic, musical timbre of a Yeats poem, but it doesn't. It's barf bags and a roof rack crammed full of vacuum-packed pillows, because that is the nature of things.'

Many others of Irish descent have spoken of how Irish they continue to feel. Colin Farrell has said that 'being Irish is very much a part of who I am. I take it everywhere with me.' The actress Lara Flynn Boyle risks slipping into Oirish sentimentality when she says 'that's what the holidays are for – for one person to tell the stories and another to dispute them. Isn't that the Irish way?'

And, of course, being Irish leads to some strange passions. In 2015, when Brian Nooney from Mullingar realized that it was impossible to buy his favourite comfort food (the Birds Eye potato waffle) in Australia, he set up a Facebook

page to campaign for the company to stock the product in the area – and its popularity did in fact persuade them that there was enough demand from expats. Unfortunately, after a couple of years the waffle was withdrawn in 2017 and one Irish mammy took extreme action. Tizzie Hall, who had emigrated from Dublin to Victoria, stockpiled as much of the remaining stock as she could before it disappeared. She said: 'We bought 1,300 but I could eat them for breakfast, lunch and dinner and my lads love them too. I tell you what, if Kerrygold gets pulled from the Australian market I'll be heading home.'

'Ireland used to be eight people without teeth fighting over a bag of crisps in Grogan's pub. Then we got rich and it costs 400,000 euros to live in a tree.'

DYLAN MORAN

MRS O'LEARY'S COW

Many Irish emigrants faced prejudice in their new country, which bonded them together and maintained their Irish identity. The Great Chicago Fire of 1871 was quickly blamed on 'Mrs O'Leary's cow', which had supposedly kicked over a lantern in a barn full of hay, though historians have subsequently argued that this was a bit of scapegoating driven by anti-Irish feeling. And, as the title of John Lydon's autobiography reminds us, it's only a few decades since landlords in London displayed signs saying 'No Irish, No Blacks, No Dogs'. As the comic Tommy Tiernan says: 'We Irish don't invade countries. We infest them.'

The statistics are remarkable – in the nineteenth century alone, over eight million people moved away from Ireland. And the majority moved to America, which is why there is such a strong Irish-American population today. However, with their St Patrick's Day parades and their general ignorance of the actual history of Ireland (as opposed to the Hollywood version), they often seem very foreign indeed to an actual Irish person.

'If this humor be the safety of our race, then it is due largely to the infusion into the American people of the Irish brain.'

PRESIDENT WILLIAM HOWARD TAFT

BOUNCING BACK

It has recently become trendy to be Irish, and the Irish in Ireland have become tired of how many second- and third-generation expats turn up with strange ideas of what Irishness actually means. Dermot Morgan (who played *Father Ted* before his tragically early death) was once ruminating on the possibility that this trendiness might wear off and he might have to return home, but he concluded that 'as long as Eamonn Holmes is working, I'm all right. If they're rounding us up and sending us home, I expect to see him on the first plane.' (Eamonn Holmes is an inexplicably popular broadcaster seen on, among other things, *Good Morning Britain* on ITV.)

'One was definitely Irish . . . The second man was unmistakably American. It wasn't so much his tan or dark hair that gave him away as how he held himself. He had an eager air, as though the world was full of possibility. Irish people never looked like that.'

RACHAEL ENGLISH

WHEN IRISH EYES ARE SMILING

Of course, it's hard to define what Irish people actually look like. The original Celtic red-headed strain was supplemented long ago by darker hair from the remnants of the Spanish Armada, and other traits from immigrants and visitors from the Vikings onwards. A character in Paul Murray's book *Skippy Dies* describes someone as Irish-looking, 'by which she meant a collection of indistinct features – pale skin, mousy hair, general air of ill-health – that combine to mysteriously powerful romantic effect.' And the Irish look (whatever it be) still pops up right around the world.

One in ten Australians is said to have some Irish blood, and because Ireland is within the European Union, the look is definitely spreading. The sense of humour doesn't always travel, mind. If you're in Italy, you're not going to get many laughs out of the locals using the Flann O'Brien line: 'Rome wasn't built in AD'.

And talking of travel and building, the Irish were famous for building railways and roads in England and America, while others appeared on building sites. But the degree to which the expats in each country identify as Irish is testament to the complex relationships between the different nationalities. As ever, such relationships find their way into jokes. Forget the English jokes belittling the 'thick' Irish navvies because some invert that traditional trope and highlight the Irish history of erudition and literature. For instance …

An Irishman went for a job on a building site, and the foreman warned him that he'd have to answer some difficult questions.

'Sure,' said the Irishman.

'Right,' said the foreman. 'Think carefully about this

one. What's the difference between a joist and a girder.'

'Well,' said the Irishman, 'Didn't Joyce write *Ulysses* and Goethe write *Faust*?'

'You are a different kind of Irishman, Goll,'
was all she said.
'Every Irishman is a different kind of
Irishman,' said Goll.

CHARLES BRADY

FIGHTING BACK

The Irish are good at sending up other nationalities . . .

Two English lads on a stag do in Dublin decide to try and outdo each other in annoying the barman.

The first walks up to him and says: 'Hey, Paddy, did you know St Patrick was English?'

The barman calmly ignores him and keeps pulling a drink.

The second whispers, 'I know how to really wind him up.' He says: 'Hey, Paddy, did you know St Patrick was a wanker?'

The barman finally looks up and says: 'I know. Your mate just told me.'

INTERLUDE:
AN IRISH MISCELLANY

'The Irish bottle up their grievances rather than deal with them. And when they have enough saved up they either go mad or write a book.'

FRANK MCNALLY

'You'll never plough a field by turning it over in your mind.'

IRISH PROVERB

'The farmer allows walkers across the field for free, but the bull charges.'

SIGN ON A GATE ON AN IRISH FARM

'I'm really happy I went to a Catholic school because a lot of the repressive tactics they use make for great senses of humour.'

DENIS LEARY

'In Ireland there's a precedent for everything but common sense.'

BEN KIELY

'The Irish G-spot is guilt.'

CLIODHNA O'FLYNN

An Irishman was once asked to define winter. 'It's the time of year,' he explained, 'when it gets late early.'

TRADITIONAL

'I was never overweight, just under-tall. The correct height for my weight at the moment is seven feet, ten and a half inches.'

BRENDAN GRACE

'The Pope has made a fortune out of his new book,
The Pill's Grim Progress.'

FRANK CARSON

There was an old fellow at Trinity
Who solved the square root of infinity.
But it gave him such fidgets
To count up the digits
That he dropped Math and took up Divinity

Flo was fond of Ebenezer
'Eb', for short, she called her beau.
Talk of tides of love, great Caesar!
You should see them – Eb and Flo.

THOMAS DALY

'Democracy means simply the bludgeoning of the people, by the people, for the people.'

OSCAR WILDE

'Ever since the IMU bailout, every child in Ireland effectively owes the government 60,000 euros at birth. Believe me, there are babies inside their mother's wombs at this very moment going, "I'm not coming out!"'

KEITH FARNAN

'The priest at my school used to follow us to dances. He'd come between me and the girl I was dancing with and say "You have to keep this far apart" as he indicated his ruler. Presumably he was imagining my penis to be the same size. I always thought he was an incredible optimist.'

DAVE ALLEN

'Irish people don't dance. The just stand in the same place and eventually start jumping up and down as if they hated the floor.'

KEITH FARNAN

'Weather and sport were invented to allow Irish family members to converse at great length with each other without saying anything dangerous.'

DAVID SLATTERY

'There's no such thing as fame in Ireland because everyone knows everyone. There aren't six degrees of separation between people, only one. They say things like, "He's not famous. Sure, my girlfriend f**ked his brother."'

DES BISHOP

'When the Irishman heard that curiosity killed the cat he said: "What was he curious about?"'

DAVE ALLEN

'The shovels haven't arrived, and until they do, you'll have to lean on each other.'

NOTICE ON AN IRISH BUILDING SITE

'Christopher Columbus, as everyone knows, is honoured by posterity because he was the last to discover America.'

JAMES JOYCE

'Reality isn't for everyone; it's something only Lutherans can enjoy.'

MARY MCDONNELL

CHAPTER NINE

BACON AND CABBAGE

Irish Cooking

'It's a terrible world where your child says to you
"Daddy, is this organic?" I grew up with Angel
Delight. That was the main course.'

DYLAN MORAN

Irish cuisine is at a crossroads. On the one hand you still have the traditional Irish staples of colcannon, soda bread, breakfast rolls, boxty and Irish stew, and on the other hand the hipster eateries of Dublin (and beyond) increasingly feature street food from around the world, minimalist dishes of strange cuts of meat served with froth and dazzling arrays of vegetation that would have been unheard of on an Irish restaurant table a generation ago.

> *'The humble cornflake is sometimes maligned.*
> *Someone once told me there's more nutrition and*
> *fibre in the cardboard box than the cereal.'*
>
> PAUL KILDUFF

LAUGHTER IS BRIGHTEST WHERE FOOD IS BEST

Hugh Leonard was describing the food of old when he wrote: 'Once, in Cork city, a beaming waitress set in front of me a plate awash with watery beans and peas, potatoes with the consistency of a bar of Lifebuoy soap and a steak which not only resembled a mummified hand from the crypt of St Michan's but actually moved as I stared at it.'

And it is true that Irish food used to be fairly basic. Traditional Irish jokes tend to refer to potatoes, beer and whiskey as the 'three food groups of Ireland', or resort to other variations on the riff of potatoes and booze. Terry

Eagleton once unkindly commented that 'Ireland's main contribution to cosmopolitan cooking is lard, in which they dip more or less everything except their toenails – and even that's not certain.' And Brian Friel once wrote of the Irish language: 'Yes, it is a rich language, lieutenant, full of the mythologies of fantasy and hope and self-deception – a syntax opulent with tomorrows. It is our response to mud cabins and a diet of potatoes.'

But the bacon and cabbage era is long gone. I recently attended a funeral where the traditional ham sandwiches were replaced by smoked salmon canapés and, instead of a piece of cake, I was offered some almond tiramisu. Food in Ireland has clearly moved on from the nineteenth to the twenty-first century without having dallied for long in the twentieth century. Mind you, the elderly gentleman sat next to me was not best pleased to see the range of salads on offer: 'If God had intended us to eat leaves, he'd have given us hooves and horns.'

A salad used to be a bit of lettuce and cress or cucumber (without dressing, of course), left on the side of the plate purely for decorative purposes, to be discarded later. It was only in the posher circles that Oscar Wilde's comment on salad would even have made sense: 'To make a good salad is to be a brilliant diplomatist – the problem is entirely the same in both cases. To know exactly how much oil one must put with one's vinegar.'

Oil! Olive oil! Isn't that for the bathroom cabinet, to be used for cleaning out the waxy ears? What's it doing on a salad, for God's sake?

However, there is still comfort to be found in some of the old dishes. Des Bishop says that 'Irish parents assume you'll realize they love you because they feed you every day. The Irish way to say "I love you" is "Get the stew into you now, good man."'

James Joyce was once in the company of Samuel Beckett, listening to some literary types droning on about their theories, when he said: 'If only they'd talk about turnips.' If only indeed.

'A stewardess of Aer Lingus asks a passenger if he'd like lunch. "What's on the menu?" he asks. "Well, there's chicken, beef, salmon or duck." "What's the duck like?" "It's like a chicken but it swims."'

TERRY WOGAN

THE USB CAKE

When Karen Moroney's daughter Layla-Valentina was approaching her second birthday, the Limerick mother decided that the perfect cake would be one featuring her child's favourite TV character, Peppa Pig. She transferred a single image of the cute character onto a USB stick and handed this over at the bakery for their guidance. However, when she arrived to pick up the cake, she was shocked to find the results. Under the icing message, 'Happy 2nd Birthday Layla-Valentina', there was a giant image of . . . a

USB stick. Karen said: 'The cake tasted fab and we all had a laugh in the end, and we got the price of the cake back!' Her husband Kevin added: 'We are laughing about it now. It's a comedy show.'

DON'T TOUCH THE FOOD!

There is an obvious connection between food and the emotions, with Joe O'Connor saying 'I can never trust a person who doesn't love food. It's a sign of meanness of spirit.' Oscar Wilde once suggested that after a good dinner one can forgive anybody, even one's own relations. And if you ever want to see panic on the face of an Irish mammy, then the quickest way is to decline her offer of food.

It was once commonplace for many Irish people to regard anything other than the most basic food as an unwanted interruption in their drinking schedules. When Richard Harris, terminally ill from his excesses – mostly the consumption of alcohol – was being taken from the Savoy Hotel to a waiting ambulance, he pushed himself up off his stretcher and shouted to the entire foyer: 'It was the food. Don't touch the food!'

Today, that attitude has softened to a more nostalgic view that the old meat and potato kinds of dishes are superior and one should be wary of salads or anything involving quinoa or ancient grains. Dan Buckley suggests, for instance, that 'broccoli, green beans and asparagus can only be enjoyed by nerds, nuns and people with bowel disorder'. And Ardal O'Hanlon says, 'I make a lot of jokes about vegetarians

in my act but most of them don't have the strength to protest.' You need to be careful with the stodgy food if you are watching your weight, though: as they say, 'the journey of a thousand pounds begins with a single burger'.

'Give up the maple syrup, Beyoncé. I want to see you eating pizza like the rest of us. And wearing big knickers to hold your stomach in afterwards.'

MARTINA DEVLIN

OYSTERS AND CHAMPAGNE

There are, of course, some traditional foods that are not too stodgy. 'It was a bold man who first swallowed an oyster,' as Jonathan Swift observed, but they are now a delicacy to be savoured. (If you like the seafood, that is – as Flann O'Brien said: 'One man's food is another man's *poisson*'.)

The West of Ireland is famed for having some of the best oysters in the world. A trip there is best arranged around one of the annual oyster festivals, but in the modern world of the euro, oysters don't come cheap. P. J. O'Rourke's advice is sound: 'Never serve oysters in a month that has no paycheck in it.'

But, whether you go for a fancy oyster bar, an old-school Irish stew at home, some hearty fare in a pub or a thirteen-course taster menu with champagne in the trendiest eatery in Dublin, you can rest assured that the company and the craic will be as important as the food. Which brings me to a sign, recently spotted on a shop door in Kinsale: 'Out for lunch. If not back by five, out for dinner also.'

'I brought a woman to a restaurant. She said, "I guess I'll have a steak." I said, "Guess again."'

BRENDAN O'CARROLL

CHAPTER TEN

CRACKPOTS
AND CHARMERS

Irish Eccentrics

'We are all born mad. Some remain so.'

SAMUEL BECKETT

Ireland has had more than its fair share of eccentrics. When Jonathan Swift wrote his will he left money for the foundation of a madhouse in Ireland on the basis that 'no nation needs it so much'. Of course, the oddness started way back in history when the religious life led to a profusion of odd scholars and monks who undertook peculiar practices such as becoming hermits, living in forests or whipping themselves with nettles. One of my favourites is St Kevin who was, at least, kind to animals – he once prayed in one position for so long that a blackbird made its nest in his cupped hands.

'I'm Irish. We think sideways.'

SPIKE MILLIGAN

ODDITIES, MALE AND FEMALE

The rural life also produced some strange people, such as Robert Cook, a seventeenth-century farmer in County Waterford. He had some odd ideas about colour, wearing nothing but white clothes and not allowing a black cow or horse to cross his land. He was also a vegan at a time when it was not remotely trendy, refusing to wear or eat anything made from an animal. He was even kind to foxes – when his staff caught one that had attacked his chickens, he made them let it go after giving them a lecture about how the bible tells us that 'Thou shalt not kill'.

By the eighteenth century, the towns and cities were also known for a variety of peculiar characters. A lady known by her fellow Dubliners as the 'Female Oddity' was reputed to eat some strange things: it was said that 'a fricassee of frogs and mice is her delight'. The inventor Richard Pokrich wanted all Irishmen to own their own pair of wings and had a complex plan to turn Ireland's bogs into vineyards, where the finest wine would be made. And Judge Norbury once allowed a guilty murderer to go free on the basis that 'I hanged six men at last Tipperary assizes who were innocent, so I'll let off this poor devil now to square matters.'

Vesian Pick was a Huguenot and a compulsive political wheeler dealer, who managed to get himself elected mayor of Cork in the late eighteenth century. He was knighted for helping resist an attempted French landing at Bantry Bay. He is remembered fondly for his somewhat erratic ways, and his letter to the Lord Lieutenant during the failed invasion started: 'I am writing this letter with a sword in one hand and a pistol in the other . . .'

Many notable eccentrics were members of the Anglo-Irish aristocracy. For instance, Mary Monckton, the wife of the Seventh Earl of Cork, was known to give wonderful parties but she was a difficult guest because she was such a compulsive kleptomaniac. She was noted for stealing silver cutlery in particular, but once managed to make off with a pet hedgehog concealed in her handbag.

Meanwhile, the Third Marquis of Waterford was a prankster on a large scale. He once took several casks of

gin into town and stood giving out large measures to anyone who was, in his opinion, deserving of his 'charity'. The result was a drunken riot and his arrest for provoking it. He also ended up in court for racing his horse too fast in a built-up area. He arrived at the trial on horseback, rode up the steps of the court and demanded that the horse be called as a witness, as it was the only one who actually knew the speed. He died in 1859, perhaps not surprisingly, after falling off a speeding horse.

'If you present my father with a statement such as "Grass is green", he's quite likely to reply, "Ah, yes, but what do you mean by green?"'

EMMA DONOGHUE

THE WORLD'S BIGGEST BALLOON

In the nineteenth century, the aristocratic resident of Stratford Lodge in Baltinglass, Benjamin O'Neill Stratford, had an obsession with creating the world's biggest balloon. In the 1830s he built a huge hangar on his property. He was deeply paranoid and employed only one servant, who was sworn to secrecy, while having his meals delivered by coach. In 1856 the balloon was ready for its maiden flight, which was to be from Baltinglass to Paris, where Stratford had bought a field to land on.

Unfortunately, there was a huge fire at the Lodge. When the locals tried to extinguish the flames he told them not to bother, just save the balloon, but they were unable to do so and he was left with his dreams in ashes. He moved to Spain to lick his wounds and lived in hotel rooms, where he refused to have his dirty crockery taken away and kept ordering meals from room service. When there was no space left in a room, he would move to another, leaving the previous one in a terrible state of disarray.

*'Success consists of getting up just one
more time than you fall.'*
OLIVER GOLDSMITH

A GLORIOUS NEW WORLD

Modern Ireland also has its share of interesting people. Father Neil Horan (born 1947) is an ex-priest often referred to as the 'Grand Prix Priest' or the 'Dancing Priest', with a strong interest in prophecy. He has published ebooks such as *A Glorious New World Very Soon to Come* and *Christ Will Soon Take Power From All Governments*, which predict

the end of the world. To promote this belief, he has interrupted numerous sporting occasions, including the 2003 British Grand Prix and 2004 Olympics (though he was prevented from interrupting the 2004 Epsom Derby). He is also known for dancing a jig on *Britain's Got Talent*.

'Ireland is a peculiar society in the sense that it was a nineteenth-century society up to about 1970 and then it almost bypassed the twentieth century.'

JOHN McGAHERN

THE ONE, THE ONLY ...

Spike Milligan – much more than an eccentric, he was a comic genius – who did have some peculiar moments. He once said: 'My father had a profound influence on me. He was a lunatic.'

The stress of writing a weekly radio *Goon Show* did indeed lead to outbreaks of depression and manic behaviour. On one occasion, when the BBC complained about the script being late, he grabbed a knife and tried to break into Peter

Sellers' apartment. He later explained that 'I thought that if I killed Peter, it would come right. I think I just wanted them to lock me up'. And they did. He was taken to an asylum and confined in a straitjacket.

He described his humour as 'one man shouting gibberish in the face of authority, and proving by fabricated insanity that nothing could be as mad as what passes for ordinary living.' He had many odd bugbears and would often rant about the horrors of smoking, people who were late, noise, animal cruelty, overpopulation and the disappearance of Victorian lampposts.

Among his lesser known works is the anarchic *Running, Jumping and Standing Still Film*, which was directed by Dick Lester in 1959, and which does exactly what it says on the tin. At the time this was merely a surreal experiment, but it would go on to influence films such as the Beatles' *A Hard Day's Night* (also directed by Lester). Spike was once read a complimentary letter from Prince Charles on live television. His response was to describe the royal as a 'grovelling little bastard'.

---

*'Patience, thought Milligan, that word was
invented by dull buggers who couldn't
think quick enough.'*

SPIKE MILLIGAN

VAN THE MAN

Another Irish genius, Van Morrison, also has his oddities. A story from his childhood captures this in a sweet way – he was for a while a member of the Olympics, a Belfast band. Once they were on the way to a Derry gig in their minibus when they pulled up outside Van's house in East Belfast. Alfie Walsh, the singer, knocked on the door and was greeted by Van's mother. Van didn't emerge, and Alfie returned to the bus alone. 'Yer man can't play,' he said. 'His ma says he's not coming out . . . He's upstairs in his room writing poetry.'

'Ever since Stephen Dedalus, poets have tended to look at themselves as if they were angels on loan from heaven instead of scruffy old bollixes going around the place looking for a bit of inspiration.'

BRENDAN KENNELLY

CHAPTER ELEVEN

RIDING TIME

Sex and Marriage

---

*'Confession is a rare and wonderful
opportunity to be able to go in and
talk dirty to a stranger.'*

DERMOT MORGAN

We can't avoid the subject, much as the Catholic Church would like us to: the Irish have a complex set of attitudes to sex. It starts in childhood with the confessional, where you feel under so much pressure to confess to a sin that you find yourself making up something dirty.

Sex education is more widely available than it used to be and Edna O'Brien, when discussing the old days, once wrote: 'I'm an Irish Catholic so my father never discussed sex with me. We talked about sandwich meat instead.' As Dave Allen said, the Catholic Church essentially offers women the choices of 'perpetual virginity or perpetual pregnancy' due to the downer it has on contraception. And in small-town Ireland, the gossip alone can be enough to put a girl off. Maeve Binchy once said that 'if you lost your virginity in Cork, someone would be sure to find it and bring it back to your mother.'

'I didn't lose my virginity. I know exactly where I left it.'

PAT INGOLDSBY

THE GOOD UNDIES

Given that the law in Ireland derived from religious doctrine, the comedian Grainne Maguire chose a novel way to campaign in the recent abortion referendum, tweeting to TD Enda Kenny: 'Since we know how much the Irish state cares about our reproductive parts – I call my womb Ireland's littlest embassy . . . I think it's only fair that the women of Ireland let our Leader @EndaKennyTD know the full details of our menstrual cycle.'

Her campaign quickly caught on as women across Ireland took her up her suggestion: contributors included Ann Campbell (Hey @EndaKennyTD no period today but I should be ovulating soon. Not looking forward to sore breasts), Ash (@EndaKennyTD @GrainneMaguire. Not surfing the crimson wave now but i'll take an angeles style pause to think of you when i am!) and, perhaps best of all, Ciara Jane Duffy (Hey, @EndaKennyTD I'm post period so can crack out the 'good undies' now. Phew. We're safe from the Crimson Curse. This time.)

MORTAL SINNERS

The Church is famously discouraging of early sexual experimentation. Des Bishop says: 'The Church sees your sexual bits like library books on loan from God. But you're not allowed to fold the pages.' However, as Michael Redmond has pointed out: 'If you're a Catholic, you're led to believe that masturbation is a mortal sin. So, if you die without receiving confession you'll go straight to hell and eternal flames. Which is a bit of an incentive to stop wanking. But usually not enough.'

Sooner or later most people get past the regression or masturbation stage and start looking for an actual partner in crime if only because, as Sinead O'Connor says: 'The main problem with vibrators is that you can't cuddle them afterwards.'

This stage can lead to difficulties. Dylan Moran points out that 'men have the same degree of passion about women that women do about handbags'. Mary Coughlan put it more forcefully: 'The majority of Irish men are bastards and they're f**kin' useless in bed.' And there is always the danger of coming up against the wrong type of man. The late Katy French once reacted to an unfortunate encounter with Calum Best, describing him as 'an arrogant octopus with no manners who persists in trying to grab my arse'.

And even if a woman finds a nice-looking man, she may not turn out to be his type. Deirdre O'Kane's view is that 'There isn't a well-groomed man in Ireland who isn't gay. They're all rugged, like the landscape. I wouldn't know whether to f*ck them or frame them.' You could do worse than befriend them, as Pat Fitzpatrick put it: 'If you don't have a gay friend, get one as soon as you can. That way you can pepper your sentences with "My gay friend" references, which is very "now".'

Of course, it is easier for some than others: Peter O'Toole, who was of Irish descent, was once asked by an actress if there were millions of girls chasing him around the planet after he did *Lawrence of Arabia*. He replied along the lines of, 'My dear, I didn't need movies to get girls.'

126

> *'When I was a teenager I wasn't allowed any sexual freedom, so I had to settle for bondage.'*
> SINEAD MURPHY

MODERN ROMANCE

Much modern matchmaking happens, of course, via the internet, and this can lead to more mishaps and confusion. Here are a few moments from a recent survey of students, concerning their worst moments on Tinder. The first one brings to mind Mick Gorman's slightly disgraceful suggestion that 'People who knock incest usually have very ugly relatives.'

'During the Summer I was messaging this one lass on Tinder for about two weeks . . . She was my cousin.'

'My worst experience with Tinder was the time I got a Tinder notification on my phone, and then realized I don't even have Tinder . . . I was holding my boyfriend's phone.'

'Back in first year, I was a bit innocent. I genuinely thought Netflix and chill meant what it says on the tin! Needless to say, I got a right shock when I went to this one bird's house for a bit of Netflix, and she started to tie me up and everything! I nearly died.'

'The one thing they never told us about sex when I was in school was that the reason people did it was because it feels fantastic.'

GERRY RYAN

IT'S A SIN

So, in spite of all the pitfalls, somehow in the end boy meets boy, or boy meets girl, or girl meets girl, or whatever other combination it would be politically correct to mention in these gender-fluid times. And it turns out that a good time can be had after all, without God striking you down.

Father Pat Buckley once said he was often asked if it was a sin to sleep with someone. He always replied, it's not: 'It's only a sin when you stay awake'.

'People accused me of being promiscuous but sometimes I went to bed with men just for the exercise.'

NUALA O'FAOLAIN

TWENTY-FIRST-CENTURY SEX

Traditionally, there was a lot of prejudice against homosexuals in Ireland: Michael Cullen has suggested that 'heterosexuals who hate homosexuals should stop hating them,' but the prejudice was enshrined in law until fairly recently. Now of course Ireland is a different place altogether. As Graham Norton says: 'You can get gay anything now – gay tea, gay coffee, gay lager. The last one is like straight lager except it goes down easier.'

But there are still battles to be fought. Grainne McGuire responded to reports of a Canadian cop who suggested women could prevent sexual attacks if they stopped dressing like sluts: 'Who knew rapists were so picky? I've never heard of a woman on the brink of being assaulted before her assailant realized skinny jeans were doing nothing for her.'

So here we are in the twenty-first century, relatively free of the old inhibitions and hang-ups about sin, but still able to laugh at some of the old-school jokes on the subject, such as Frank Carson's, 'My wife said to me: "Why do you never talk to me when we're having sex." I said: "I don't like to wake you up."' Or Brendan O'Carroll's, 'Sex before marriage is a good idea – mainly because there's so little after it.' And Paul Ryan gives us this one: 'Will you still love him when he's no longer able to satisfy ye in bed, Josie?' 'Oh, I do, luv, I do.' But Deirdre O'Kane's more acerbic comment is perhaps funnier: 'What do clitorises and anniversaries have in common? Men always miss them.'

CHAPTER TWELVE

BETWEEN THE DEVIL AND THE DEEP BLUE SEA

Crime and Punishment

'I think there's a bit of the devil in everybody.
There's a bit of a priest in everybody, too,
but I enjoyed playing the devil more.
He was more fun.'

GABRIEL BYRNE

Of course, there are plenty of Irish people who have never had a brush with the law, who have never bent the rules and who still feel obscurely guilty, possibly because of the impact of a Catholic upbringing and being obliged to regularly think of some sins for confession. In her *What it Means to be Irish* video, Laura Fitzgibbon (aka FitznBitz) talked about things that make people truly Irish, including a bit of sunburn, the 'long goodbye' (in which neither party can stop saying 'Bye!') and feeling like you have to 'apologize for everything . . . even if you're not in the wrong'.

'One of the strangest things about life is the fact that the poor, who need money the most, are the very ones who never have it.'

FINLEY PETER DUNNE

THE CRIMINAL CLASS

Ireland has its fair share of people who are guilty of the occasional transgression, whether it be a simple case of finding a loophole in the rules and regulations or something more serious. The causes are many, and poverty can be a real motivation to finding ways to gain a bit of money here and there. As Peter O'Toole once said: 'I'm not from the working class. I'm from the criminal class.'

My great aunt Doris, who grew up in poverty and worked hard through the years of an unhappy marriage, had a bit of a windfall when she was older. She genuinely suffered from asbestosis (contracted in the factory where she worked), but managed to significantly bump up her compensation by staying up all night and smoking 100 cigarettes the night before her medical. (Warning: do not try this at home.)

This reminds me of another old story, possibly concerning compensation. At a court in Killarney, a lawyer was quizzing a farmer called Mr O'Shea, who had told the Garda officer who attended his road accident that he had never felt better in his life, though he was now claiming to have been seriously injured. The farmer's explanation: 'When the Garda arrived, he went over to my horse, who had a broken leg, and shot him. Then he went over to Darcy, my dog, who was badly hurt, and shot him. Then the policeman came across the road, gun still in hand, looked at me and said: "How are *you* feeling?" I just thought, under the circumstances, it was a wise choice of words to say: "I've never felt better in my life."'

'Are you going to come quietly, or do I have to use earplugs?'

SPIKE MILLIGAN

THE LAST RITES

Which brings me to the culture of gambling. The pool player Danny McGoorty has said that 'one of the worst things that can happen in life is to win a bet on a horse at an early age'. He also suggests another possible incentive to finding dubious ways of making a living – pure laziness: 'I have never liked working. To me a job is an invasion of privacy.' And now . . .

Two Irish gamblers go to the races. When the horses are parading before the start, they notice a priest making a fuss of one of the horses. And that horse goes on to win. This gets their attention, so they watch carefully to see which of the horses the priest makes a fuss of before the next race, and seeing him bestowing his attention on Foxy Loxy, they bet all their money on him to win. But he falls down halfway through the second circuit and has to be shot.

They retire, defeated, to the nearby pub and end up telling the story to a local. 'Ah,' he says, 'you have to learn the difference between when Reverend Murphy is blessing a horse and when he is giving it the last rites.'

'I often sit back and think, I wish I'd done that, and find out later that I already have.'

RICHARD HARRIS

A CUNNING RUSE

One Irish thief was arrested by the Greenock police in 1880. When caught, he immediately slumped and pretended to be unconscious. The Greenock police surgeon managed to prod him back into consciousness, and he was transported to the town where his offence had occurred to await trial.

He immediately escaped and fled, but was caught after a few days and, following a violent struggle, arrested. Bleeding from the mouth as a result of a blow from a baton, he was taken to the police surgeon. Unfortunately, the Greenock police had not passed on the full story to his new guards. The surgeon was fooled as the thief again feigned unconsciousness and pretended to be dying.

Indeed, his acting was so convincing that the surgeon believed he had indeed died, and laid him out in the mortuary, without his boots. Then he rushed off to inform his colleagues of the unfortunate death. When they all trooped back to the mortuary to pay their respects they found that the thief had, yet again, escaped.

'Being Irish, he had an abiding sense of tragedy, which sustained him through temporary periods of joy.'

W. B. YEATS

WHEN IS A CRIME NOT A CRIME?

Sheer devilment can often be brought about by a drop of alcohol, and even the most idyllic of rural locations see the practical jokers and pranksters finding ways to amuse themselves. The road sign in County Kerry that reads 'Inch – 1 mile' is still being stolen on a regular basis.

For whatever reason, crime is an ever-present part of everyday life. Joe Carmody has said: 'We're told the streets of Dublin aren't safe any more. Really? I think the streets are very safe indeed. I have a few problems with the people that are on them, though.'

Assuming that the government doesn't take Kevin Marron's advice – 'The government should nationalize crime. That way it wouldn't pay.' – a minority of the Irish nation will continue to have occasional skirmishes with the law. Naturally, this often leads to a negative opinion of the police. Eugene O'Neill said that 'when St Patrick drove all the snakes out of Ireland, they all swam to New York and joined the police force.'

'Why do they put photos of criminals up in post offices? Are we supposed to write to them?'

MICHAEL CULLEN

A FAIR DEAL

Judge Seamus Hughes, of Athlone's District Court, is known for having passed down some of the more inventive sentences in Ireland's courts. He once found a young Tullamore artist guilty of stealing whiskey and shotguns. In sentencing, he instructed the defendant to 'do an artist's sketch of the courtroom, focusing, in particular, on the practitioners of the court'. He wanted the artist to 'work hard at this' so it would be ready as 'a Christmas present for the December 19 sitting of the court'.

EVEN WORSE THAN THE POLICE

Patrick Kavanagh once said that 'there is something wrong with a work of art if it can be understood by a policeman'. And Norman Mailer once asked Brendan Behan if he had a police escort when he returned to Dublin. 'Yeah,' said Behan, 'but I'm usually handcuffed to the bastards!' Behan also claimed that 'I was court-martialled in my absence and sentenced to death in my absence, so I said they could shoot me in my absence.'

Any story that starts out with the police will often go on to involve lawyers. And they get an even worse rap. During the boom years, the politician Pat Rabbitte memorably expressed his dislike of the breed: 'Of all the cubs being suckled by the Irish Tiger, by far the fattest, sleekest and best nurtured are the lawyers.' Patrick Murray concurs, saying that 'a lawyer will do anything to win a case – even tell the truth'.

The general opinion is that lawyers are not much better than the criminals they represent. Seamus O'Leary says: 'My brother is a criminal lawyer. Aren't they all?' But the problem is that lawyers feed on badly made laws, and the laws are often badly made for a reason. As Pat Shortt says: 'Beneath every law lurks a lovely loophole.'

'You might as well employ a boa constrictor as a tape measure as go to a lawyer for legal advice.'

OLIVER ST JOHN GOGARTY

CUTE HOORS

And this brings us to the politicians. Irish politicians are a motley crew – 'cute hoors' the lot of them – it has been said that their smiles are like 'moonlight on a tombstone'. Daniel O'Connell described an honest politician as, 'one who, when bribed, stays bribed'. One newspaper in Ireland was asked to retract a story that claimed that half the local council were crooks. They responded by running the headline: 'Half the Council are NOT crooks.'

So, it's not surprising to find many finely honed insults being fired in the direction of the politicians. For instance, Sean Kilroy suggests that 'first God made morons, imbeciles and complete idiots. That was practice. Then he made politicians.'

And Pat Shortt has described them as being 'like nappies. They should be changed often. And usually for the same reason.'

'The Irish legal system is weighted heavily in favour of the Church. As far as I know, it's still illegal to hit a nun.'

IAN MACPHERSON

YOUR ENEMIES' ENEMIES

An old Irish proverb is 'here's health to your enemies' enemies!' The problem is that the enemy of a politician is usually another politician. Joe Duffy once described choosing between Fianna Fail, Fine Gael and Labour as being like 'choosing between jumping from the thirteenth, fourteenth or fifteenth storey of a skyscraper'. And David Kenny was writing about Fianna Fail politicians in particular when he described them as being 'likely to say something like "We must tighten our belts for the lean times ahead" before one of them unbuckles his own and ravishes your sister.'

You can generally trust Flann O'Brien to come up with a pithy phrase or two. He once wrote that 'our ances-tors believed in magic, prayer, trickery, browbeating and bullying. I think it would be fair to sum that up as "Irish politics".' So, a curse on all their houses. But if you are feeling hemmed in by a combination of chancers, scoundrels, the police, the dodgy lawyers and the crooked politicians of this world, then you may need to remember Oscar Wilde's advice: 'Always forgive your enemies. Nothing annoys them so much.'

'I read in the paper that Bertie Ahern is going to "buck up" the Irish economy. There has to be a misprint there somewhere.'

MAUREEN POTTER

CHAPTER THIRTEEN

TALL TALES

Irish Literary Life

For the young Gaels of Ireland
Are the lads that drive me mad,
For half their words need footnotes
And half their rhymes are bad.

ARTHUR GUITERMAN

The Irish are a nation of storytellers, so it is not so surprising that they have such a rich and thriving literary culture. And, of course, the art of telling tales can sometimes mean twisting facts to fit a narrative. Richard Brinsley Sheridan once said of a contemporary that he was 'indebted to his memory for his jests and to his imagination for his facts'. There's also a great story about Bono appearing at a U2 concert in Dublin – in between songs, he slowly starts clapping his hands and says 'Every time I clap my hand, a child dies'. To which a lone voice from the audience replies: 'So stop fecking doing it then!' This is actually an embellishment of an urban myth that keeps getting passed on because it skewers Bono's pomposity so nicely.

'I mean to say, whether a yarn is tall or small I like to hear it well told. I like to meet a man that can take in hand to tell a story and not make a balls of it while he's at it. I like to know where I am, do you know. Everything has a beginning and an end.'

FLANN O'BRIEN

WHERE STRANGE TALES BEGIN

Charles Haughey once said that 'Ireland is where strange tales begin and happy endings are possible', and as a politician he certainly was no stranger to a tall tale or two. But politicians aren't the only ones whose craft relies on performance and anecdote. Sean O'Casey may have said that all the world's a stage and most of us are desperately unrehearsed, but the raconteurs of a traditional Irish pub are often accomplished performers who treat the pub floor as their own personal stage. Maeve Binchy once wrote that 'a good way to write a novel is to go into a pub, sit down and listen'.

On the whole, the Irish are a well-read nation, who are proud of their literary heritage. Even a simple sign on a café door in Mayo recently employed a literary reference: 'Gone to lunch, back in five minutes – Godot.' But respect for literature is not ubiquitous. My wife's Irish granddad once visited and surveyed our combined collection of books with wry amusement.

'Have you read all them books?' he said.

'A lot of them . . .' she replied, tentatively.

'You want to get a job,' he replied.

'I want to write a bestseller, so I've decided to call my book Harry Potter and the Da Vinci Book of Sudoku.*'*

DAVID O'DOHERTY

THE LIT CRIT BRIGADE

The urge to write can come from a variety of things. It might be inspired by a childhood, although as Frank McCourt points out: 'As far as literary inspiration goes, a happy childhood isn't worth a f*ck.' It can also be rooted in the desire to be famous, although this can be a wild goose chase.

It's worth bearing in mind that the writing life is not an easy one. Clare Boylan has said that 'the most important thing a writer should have is a partner with a steady income'. And Ed Byrne has noted that 'no one ever committed suicide while reading a good book, but many have tried while trying to write one'.

Humour has been a big part of Irish literature since the earliest times. *The Vision of Mac Conglinne*, which was written in the eleventh or twelfth century, is an early example of a parody. It tells the story of Aniér Mac Conglinne, a scholar from Armagh. His quest is to rescue King Cathal Mac Finnguine from the demon of gluttony, and while trying he dreams of a land made entirely of food:

The fort we reached was beautiful,
With works of custards thick,
Beyond the loch.
New butter was the bridge in front,
The rubble dyke was wheaten white,
Bacon the palisade.

Stately, pleasantly it sat,
A compact house and strong.
Then I went in:
The door of it was dry meat,
The threshold was bare bread,
Cheese-curds the sides.

Smooth pillars of old cheese,
And sappy bacon props
Alternate ranged;
Fine beams of mellow cream,
White rafters – real curds,
Kept up the house.

Of course, there are some great Irish writers, and even the most intimidating literary giants have their humorous side. The American critic Ezra Pound once decried the fuss being made about James Joyce's new book: 'Only a new cure for the clap can possibly justify all the circumambient peripherization of *Finnegans Wake*. It's just one long spelling mistake.' But Joyce himself was willing to make fun of his own creation, saying: 'I wrote *Finnegans Wake* to keep the lit crit brigade in sinecures for the rest of the century'.

'*Definition of an "Irish fact": That which tells you not what is the case but what you want to hear.'*

HUGH KENNER

EVERY BONE IN THEIR HEADS

The bane of every writer is, of course, the critic. Daniel Day-Lewis has said that, 'Before I became an actor I had a brief but disastrous flirtation with journalism. I was offered a book to review once, I read it twice, thought about it for three weeks, and then decided I had nothing at all to say about it.'

If only all critics were so circumspect. Lee Dunne dismisses their views thus: 'I've never had any time for literary critics. I wouldn't pay too much attention to a fella who couldn't get a hard-on telling me how to go about getting laid.' While Eugene O'Neill, the American playwright who was the son of an Irish immigrant actor, said: 'Critics? I love every bone in their heads.'

'When Keats was my age he had been dead for eleven years. This clearly gave him an unfair advantage with the critics.'

JOE O'CONNOR

CRAMP HER LARYNX . . .

The playwright J. M. Synge was once infuriated by the sister of an enemy who disapproved of *The Playboy of the Western World*. His very literary response was to write a poem cursing her:

Lord, confound this surly sister,
Blight her brow with blotch and blister,
Cramp her larynx, lung and liver,
In her guts a galling give her.
Let her live to earn her dinners
In Mountjoy with seedy sinners:
Lord, this judgment quickly bring,
And I'm your servant, J. M. Synge.

I COULD HARDLY BELIEVE
MY EYES

Those who can't write become critics. Those who can't even become critics are mere journalists, a breed that is even more despised by many writers, fairly or unfairly. George Bernard Shaw wrote that, 'Newspapers are unable, seemingly, to discriminate between a bicycle accident and the collapse of civilization'. And Oscar Wilde gives us this gem: 'There is much to be said in favour of modern journalism. By giving us the opinions of the uneducated it keeps us in touch with the ignorance of the community.' No matter how true that may have been in his day, the tabloid newspapers of today have outdone their forebears.

Irish newspapers have had their fair share of foot-in-mouth moments, such as the sub-editor who wasn't concentrating when writing the headline 'Massive Jobs Blow for Belmullet' but transposed 'Jobs' and 'Blow'. And there's the editor who placed a picture of a smiling redheaded recipient of an award under a news story, which had the headline: 'F**king Ginger Irish B**tard'.

One slow news day in County Sligo saw the local newspaper reporting that a hat had been found in a tree in Carney Village. It continued: 'The head garment, which is green with a white bobble, was discovered last Sunday by a local resident. "I could hardly believe my eyes when I saw it up there. I got it down with a stick and put it on the fence post opposite Laura's pub."' An appeal was issued for the hat's owner to retrieve it by 6 December, after which, 'it will be destroyed'.

Finally, my favourite Irish newspaper front page comes from the *Metro Herald*, which greeted the first sunny day of the year with the magnificent headline 'Yellow Object Spotted In Sky'.

*'There are as many ways to "get into journalism" as there are to f*ck up your life in general.'*
DECLAN LYNCH

GENUINE NEWSPAPER HEADLINES

POLICE DISCOVER CRACK IN AUSTRALIA

DRUNK GETS NINE MONTHS IN VIOLIN CASE

DEAD WOMAN MAY HAVE DISTURBED BURGLAR

LUCKY MAN SEES FRIENDS DIE

20-YEAR-OLD FRIENDSHIP ENDS AT ALTAR

Deaf Mute Gets New Hearing at Court

MOUNTING PROBLEMS FOR YOUNG COUPLES

WOMAN IN SUMO WRESTLER SUIT ASSAULTED HER EX-GIRLFRIEND IN A GAY BAR AFTER SHE WAVED AT A MAN DRESSED AS A SNICKERS BAR

CHICK-LIT AND FAT FROGS

The modern literary world is a different place to the rather high-falutin' authors of the past. There are, of course, still some writers with artistic aspirations, hence John Broderick's 'I'm sick and tired of novelists who write novels about novelists writing novels about novelists.' But some of the most successful writers around now are in genres such as chick-lit. This is Pat Fitzpatrick's satirical response: 'Encouraged by the money Marian Keyes and Cecelia Ahern make with chick-lit, I'm writing a boy-lit novel. It's the story of Malcolm, a successful twenty-something who's having trouble finding a woman. All they want to do is drink Fat Frogs and flash their boobs while he likes to cry over nothing and sometimes go to fortune tellers.'

Even the format of books is changing. The rise of the ebook has led to alarm that the bookshops of the future may be dystopian digital nightmares. J. P. Donleavy had a different reason for scepticism: 'Electronic books are a bad thing because they cannot be accumulated on shelves to remind you of your past, to impress your neighbours and colleagues, and to help prevent divorces thanks to the sheer bother of arguing over who owns what.'

CHAPTER FOURTEEN

TOO OLD TO BE YOUNG AND TOO YOUNG TO BE OLD

Family Life – and Death

'I'm having difficulty getting the doctors around here to sign the appropriate form.'

SPIKE MILLIGAN, ON ATTEMPTING TO
CELEBRATE HIS EIGHTIETH BIRTHDAY
WITH A 12,000-FOOT SKYDIVE

There comes a time in your life when you look at your friends and realize how old they are. You look at the television and realize that most of the politicians are younger than you. You meet someone who you think looks old and then find out they are younger than you. And eventually you might even bring yourself to look in the mirror and realize that maybe you're getting on a bit, too. Ah well . . .

'He was a good family man. Everywhere he went, he started a new family.'

LIAM O'REILLY

YOUNG AT HEART

The hardest thing of all is realizing that you are now older than your parents were when you were a kid, you know, when you thought they were ancient and not worth paying any attention to. It starts happening at the age Sean Hughes is talking about: 'I've hit that age now when I'm too old to be young and too young to be old. It's the age when you start being invited to dinner parties.' And then the whole relentless process just carries on from there. One option would be to take Frank Hall's advice: 'If you're going to lie about your age, do it in the opposite direction than most people. If you're thirty-nine tell them you're fifty-five and they'll think you look brilliant.'

An old Irish saying is, 'You've got to do your own growing,

no matter how tall your father was'. It's making the point that we all find our own way through life but may not end up with the same kind of family situation as our parents. If, however, you have taken the marriage and kids route, there is plenty of traditional Irish advice for you, as well as bad jokes like this Tom O'Connor one: 'The most difficult years of marriage are those following the wedding.'

'Marriage is when two people are joined together to become one desperately boring person.'

ARDAL O'HANLON

MUTUAL MISUNDERSTANDING

As Oscar Wilde puts it: 'The proper basis for marriage is mutual misunderstanding.' And family life in general rests on a variety of unspoken rules that are designed to stop us finding out too much about each other. As David Slattery says: 'The general rule at Irish family gatherings is that you should only discuss topics in which you have no real interest.' Not that family gatherings are as common as they once were. Ardal O'Hanlon complains that, 'There were only three occasions in life when you'd find our whole family together. Family wedding, family funeral or I brought home a bag of chips.'

*'Here's to you and yours, and to mine and ours, and
if mine and ours ever come across to you and yours,
I hope you and yours will do as much for
mine and ours as mine and ours have done
for you and yours!'*

TRADITIONAL IRISH BLESSING

THE LITTLE CHISELERS

And won't someone think of the children? What are we doing to the poor little buggers as we thrash through our mid-life crises and continue to improvise parenting skills on the spot. Jason Byrne has some sympathy, saying: 'I have an eight-year-old child and he's a bit deranged because he's been living with me for eight years.'

At first, children are great fun. Dylan Moran says: 'Children are just midget drunks. They greet you in the morning by kneeing you in the face and talking gibberish.' But they will insist on growing up. You eventually reach the point where, as the old joke has it, they stop asking you where they came from and start refusing to tell you where they're going.

The politician Máire Geoghegan-Quinn has expressed that paranoid thought that many parents of teenagers have had from time to time. 'When your kid is about fifteen or sixteen, someone takes them away and replaces them with a lookalike that's an absolute swine. When the kid is about twenty or twenty-one, they do another swap and you get your own child back.'

And as the children grow up, it is hard to remember that they are indeed grown-ups and can fight their own battles. Dan Sheehan (who numbers Flann O'Brien among his ancestors) wrote the hilarious book *Restless Souls* about 'suicide, the war in Sarajevo, and post traumatic stress disorder'. He subsequently said: 'My father has just retired . . . and he's taken to going to bookshops and talking loudly about how good my book is. He's very enthusiastic, which I appreciate. But Dad, please, *please* stop.'

'I grew up among strong women, so I know what it's like to be loved and humiliated in a heartbeat.'

CHRIS O'DOWD

THE TEARS OF THE WORLD

And, of course, not all marriages survive, especially now that divorce in Ireland is legal. Cathy Kelly captures part of the underlying problem when she writes that 'women are programmed to think they're the only screw-up in the universe and men are programmed to think they're the smartest creatures in the universe'.

It may be true that 'Irish men only cry when they're trying to assemble Ikea furniture', but the challenges of maintaining a marriage can, in the end, make emotional wrecks of many of us, at which point even the most steadfast of Irish men may find other reasons to cry. Alternatively, the start of the end may come when an Irish woman looks in the mirror or catches on to the way she is shouting for the children to wake up, and that 'Breakfast won't make itself, will it?' and realizes it has finally happened: she has become an Irish mammy!

Hal Roach once said: 'You only have to mumble a few words in a church to get married and a few words in your sleep to get divorced.' But many marriages do stumble on, in spite of these challenges. Hopefully Joe Cuddy was joking when he claimed, 'I'm pretty sure that my wife would divorce me if she could find some way of doing it that wouldn't make me happy.'

'When I got divorced I went through the various stages of grieving: anger, denial, dancing around my settlement cheque.'

MAURA KENNEDY

THE PATIENCE OF ANGELS

Richard Harris's wife Elizabeth was known for a long time for her patience in the face of his love of alcohol and hellraising. One Saturday lunchtime, Harris left the house with a friend to go to a football match.

'When will I see you?' asked Elizabeth.

'Tuesday,' he replied. 'And it might be in the police courts.'

Her patience did have limits, however. Another time, Harris found himself being ejected from a London pub at closing time and promptly caught a train, purely so that he could keep drinking at a bar. He had no idea where he would end up, but found himself in Leeds, completely drunk. He wandered the streets and chucked a stone at the first window where he saw lights on.

The furious owner marched out of the house, but Harris was lucky: he was a fan of the actor and invited him in. Four days later, with Harris still drinking, the owner's wife phoned Elizabeth and said: 'I've got your husband.'

'Good,' she replied. 'Keep him.'

'I had a rough childhood. I was breastfed
by my father.'

JAMES McKEAN

FEATHERY STROKERS

When marriages do fail, men deal with being newly single in middle age in particularly undignified ways. Some, noticing that 'old men' have been supplanted by the 'new man', attempt to learn how to simulate modern manners. Marian Keyes has one of her characters deriding both new men and their imitators as 'Feathery Strokers', a category that includes 'Men who didn't eat red meat . . . Men who noticed your shoes and handbags . . . Men who said pornography was exploitation of women . . . Men who stayed friends with their ex-girlfriends . . . especially if they called them their "ex-partner" . . . And men who did Pilates.' (She does also note that the men who described pornography as exploitative might just be liars.)

'Marriage is the triumph of imagination over intelligence. Second marriage is the triumph of hope over experience.'

OSCAR WILDE

NANA AND GRANDA

And, at some point, you may find you're becoming a grandparent. Kids are so much easier the second time around, mainly because you can give them back when you get bored. Liz Kavanagh has written: 'My grandchildren are so wonderful, I should have had them first.'

So, you eventually find yourself married, single, remarried or whatever, then on the verge of old age. Have you heard the Irish blessing? 'May you live as long as you want, and never want as long as you live.' The question is, how long do you actually want to live?

Dylan Moran claims to be looking forward to old age, purely so that he can lean over in a restaurant and say: 'You know what I just did? I just pissed myself, you deal with it, now carry on telling me about your job or divorce or whatever the f*ck it is. I'm not really listening to you, to be honest, which one are you? Siobhan or Simon? I can never tell.'

Others find more impressive ways to deal with ageing. Eileen Maguire, an eighty-six-year-old great-grandmother, found herself going viral after joining in with the sledging on Sweeney's Hill in Rathpeacon, County Cork. She was accompanied by her grandson Jack who reported that, 'She was screeching like a banshee going down the hill. It was so funny.' Her daughter-in-law described how tough she is: 'She swims in the sea during the summer months in

Bantry, several times a day regardless of the weather – with her lipstick and everything. She won't be going to God's waiting room any time soon – she refuses point blank.'

'I find life extremely funny on a daily basis. I can't imagine looking at the world and not finding it humorous, if only in a morbid way.'

SALLY ROONEY

'IRISHMAN DIES OF STUBBORNNESS, WHISKEY'

But in the end, we know it can't be avoided – the final coda is death. David Slattery says that 'The most popular way of dying in Ireland is "peacefully". "Peacefully" covers deaths involving screaming that you don't want to go, clinging desperately to the bed-end shouting that you're still alive as they drag you towards the morgue . . .' Hopefully it won't be as bad as that.

Of course, once you're gone, people can say whatever they want about you and they will, from the wake and funeral onwards. As Dave Allen once said: 'There is no such thing as bad publicity except your own obituary.' And these days it is becoming increasingly popular to write your own obituary. One Irish-American, Chris Connors, reported his own death in 2016 under the headline 'Irishman dies of stubbornness, whiskey'. The obituary included the following vainglorious words: 'Anyone else fighting ALS and stage 4 pancreatic cancer would have gone quietly into the night, but Connors was stark naked drinking Veuve in a house full of friends and family as Al Green played from the speakers. The way he died is just like he lived: he wrote his own rules, he fought authority and he paved his own way. And if you said he couldn't do it, he would make sure he could.'

THE FINAL WORD

In the end, we live our lives knowing that one day we will be dead. And whether or not we are going to find heaven or hell, up there, down below, or in this world, we know that we'll see a mixture of good times and bad, and that all we can do is take the rough with the smooth, take the piss out of life, and enjoy the craic as long as we can. In the end, that's what Irish humour is all about.

Let's give Brendan Behan the final word: 'I want to die when I'm ninety with a mountain of pillows behind me and sixty priests and forty nuns praying fervently that I'll get into heaven.'

Amen.